A Safe Place of Work

Other Butterworths books on Safety

Safety at Work (Second edition). Edited by John Ridley

Industrial Hazard and Safety Handbook, Revised impression. Ralph W. King and John Magid

Construction, Hazard and Safety Handbook. Ralph W. King

Redgrave's Health and Safety in Factories, Second edition. His Honour Judge Ian Fife and E. Anthony Machin

Health and Safety at Work. His Honour Judge Ian Fife and E. Anthony Machin

Occupational Health Practice. Richard Schilling

Lifting Tackle Manual. D. E. Dickie and E. Short

Crane Handbook. D. E. Dickie and E Short

Handbook of Reactive Chemical Hazards, Third edition. L. Bretherick

Electrical Safety Engineering, Second edition. W. Fordham Cooper

A Safe Place of Work

D. W. B. James, MIOSH

Butterworths
London Boston Durban Singapore Sydney Toronto Wellington

All rights reserved. No part of this publication may be reproduced or transmitted in any form or by any means, including photocopying and recording without the written permission of the copyright holder, application for which should be addressed to the publishers. Such written permission must also be obtained before any part of this publication is stored in a retrieval system of any nature.

This book is sold subject to the Standard Conditions of Sale of Net Books and may not be resold in the UK below the net price given by the Publishers in their current price list.

First published 1983
  reprinted 1986

© **Butterworth & Co (Publishers) Ltd, 1983**

British Library Cataloguing in Publication Data

James, D. W. B.
  A safe place of work.
  1. Offices—Safety measures
  I. Title
  363.1'19651   HD7273

ISBN 0-408-02930-7

Library of Congress Cataloging in Publication Data

James, D. W. B. (Derek W. B.)
  A safe place of work.
  Bibliography: p.
  Includes index.
  1. Safety, Industrual. I. Title.
  T55.J34 1983   363.1'1   83-7415

ISBN 0-408-02930-7

Photoset by Butterworths Litho Preparation Department
Printed and bound in Great Britain at The Camelot Press Ltd, Southampton

Preface

The notes on these pages outline the basic philosophy of accident prevention, and summarise the main duties and responsibilities for health and safety which fall upon the shoulders of the employer.

The aim has been to offer guidance and information on a subject of considerable importance, in a way which avoids solemnity or the indulgences of esoteric jargon.

Though it is often said that 'safety is everyone's business', there is no doubt that the Manager – in whatever branch of the game – is the prime mover in the Company's accident prevention programme. He is, by virtue of his job, a leader; and it is leaders who make things happen. Accident Prevention is making things happen safely and without risk to health.

D. W. B. James

This book is dedicated to my family, my Company, and the Safety profession – in that order.

Acknowledgement

The author and publishers would like to thank The Controller, Her Majesty's Stationery Office for permission to reproduce on pages 35, 89 and 109 the extracts from various official publications.

Contents

Part 1 Let's Talk about Accidents

1.1	Responsibility – the employer's burden	1
1.2	The problem stated	4
1.3	What is an accident?	5
1.4	What is 'safety'?	8
1.5	The cost of injuries	10
1.6	Recording accidents	12
1.7	Accident investigation	19
1.8	Reporting accidents	23
1.9	Safety inspections	28

Part 2 The Legal Aspects

2.1	Health and Safety legislation	33
2.1.1	Common Law	34
2.1.2	Statute Law	36
2.2	The Factories Act 1961	37
2.3	The Health and Safety at Work etc. Act 1974	37
2.3.1	General duties and particular duties	40
2.3.1.1	Safe plant, safe systems	42
2.3.1.2	Use, handling, storage and transport	43
2.3.1.3	Information, instruction, training and supervision	44
2.3.1.4	Safe place of work, safe means of access	44
2.3.1.5	Environment and welfare provisions	45
2.3.1.6	Safety policy	46
2.3.1.7	Safety representatives and committees	47

2.3.2	Duties of employees	50
2.3.3	The Commission and the Executive	52
2.3.4	Powers of Inspectors	53
2.3.4.1	Improvement and Prohibition Notices	57
2.3.5	Approved Codes of Practice	57

Part 3 Sundry Subjects

3.1	Training-out accidents	59
3.2	Machine guarding	61
3.3	Machinery attendants	64
3.4	Highly Flammable Liquids (HFL) and LPG	66
3.5	Asbestos – the stealthy killer	70
3.6	Threshold Limit Value (TLV)	73
3.7	The problem of noise	75
3.8	The dust problem	78
3.9	Scaffolding	80
3.10	Harmful substances – informing the employee	86
3.11	Eye protection	88
3.12	Fire extinguishers	93
3.13	Fire alarms and evacuations	97
3.14	Fire prevention	99
3.15	Office safety	101
3.16	Last round-up	103

Appendix 1	Commonly Used Acts and Regulations	105
Appendix 2	Useful Reference Publications	106
Appendix 3	Journals and Other Sources	108
Appendix 4	Safety Signs	109
Appendix 5	Safety Inspection checklist	110

Index 115

Part 1
Let's Talk about Accidents

This first part of the book will deal briefly with the problem of occupational accidents, the responsibility of management in general for eliminating the causes of accidents where reasonably practicable, and the factors which relate to the maintenance of a safe place of work.

As we shall see, the term 'accident' includes other things in addition to bloodshed. In the human context it covers injury and ill-health; in the wider context it relates also to damage, lost production, fire, flood, industrial relations, and a whole list of other potential or actual situations which can be regarded as losses on the operational balance sheet of any Company.

The subject of Accident Prevention is a large and complex one. The following sections do not provide a comprehensive remedy for the problem of occupational accidents. They do, however, point to the basic procedures which should be adopted by employers.

The large major Companies will already be geared to the task and will have the expertise, the staff and the resources to carry through the necessary procedures. The smaller employer, however, should be able to adapt many of the systems referred to in these pages so that they meet the needs and the scale of his own business.

The majority of the nation's workpeople are employed by small or medium-size Companies. It is to the managers and supervisors of such Companies that this book is primarily directed.

1.1 Responsibility – the Employer's Burden

Let's begin by recognising our employer for what he is – a beast of burden.

Fierce competition, restrictive legislation, industrial relations, penal taxation, the swirling tidal forces of the marketplace, trade union practices, governmental interference, plus a host of technical and financial difficulties and considerations – all these factors conspire together to ensure that the employer has no prospect of resting peacefully on a bed of roses.

The employer lives and operates in a harsh and unforgiving world; his burden of diverse responsibilities is both leaden and permanent.

Among the catalogue of responsibilities is that of providing a safe place of work for his employees, together with safe systems of work, safe plant and machinery, adequate training and supervision, adequate welfare facilities and a range of other safety-and-health-oriented provisions. He must also ensure that whatever risk he creates within his establishment does not spill over into the outside world, to the detriment of the general public. Health and safety at the workplace, therefore, is a consideration which looms large in the employer's scheme of things, and there are plenty of organisations, bodies and individuals who will not let him forget it.

For our purpose 'the employer' may be a gigantic multinational corporation with 30 000 employees, or it may be a back-street bucket shop with two men and a part-time typist, making plastic badges – the requirements are the same, differing only in scale. What we have to do, however, is to find a more specific label for the nebulous character known as 'the employer' – we have to see him as a person whom we can recognise and identify with; as a person upon whom we can place the *responsibility* for workplace safety.

Responsibility is an awesome concept, and can have several shades of meaning. We can think in terms of legal responsibility, or moral responsibility, or professional responsibility. We can contemplate delegated responsibility, or final and absolute responsibility – the place where 'the buck stops'.

Let's first accept that the *employer* – the corporate body which is the company – is primarily responsible for what happens to its employees at their place of work. The employer, then, dictates policy; makes the rules; initiates working practices; ensures that people are properly trained; provides adequate supervision, safe plant, safe premises; maintains adequate health, safety and welfare standards.

It is the employer, therefore, who provides the stage and sets the scene for his players. His legal, moral and professional responsibilities are binding and inescapable.

Being unable, however, to be in a hundred places at once, the employer must appoint people to see that his policies are implemented and that the mechanics of his business are functioning in a properly organised and supervised manner.

Such people may be supervisors, personnel officers, engineers, production superintendents, safety officers, office administrators, section leaders, foremen, technical officers, overseers, gaffers, or any number of designations.

What they all have in common is the authority and the duty to direct people and machines in the task of getting things done. Therefore, since they are in charge of others, let's just call them *managers*, bearing in mind that there are many levels of management and that the description has a very wide coverage. Their *authority* over others invests them with a degree of *responsibility*.

With regard to health and safety at the workplace it is fair to say that, except in very exceptional cases involving gross and deliberate neglect of duty, the individual manager would suffer no legal penalties for failure to carry out his appointed task – the employer (the Company) would be prosecuted for any infringement.

The manager, however, has very real responsibilities (both moral and professional) to his employer. His responsibility to the Company for which he works is not open to question, and this extends to all aspects of his job – including accident prevention. He is, in fact, responsible for ensuring that his employer's many responsibilities are fully met.

Management at large, therefore, has to shoulder the burden of operating a safe enterprise, and it is toward management – at all its different levels – that this book is directed.

As for the employee – he is morally (and legally) responsible for his own health and safety, and for the safety of his colleagues, within the bounds of commonsense. The employee is not a mindless robot, nor a trained monkey, so he must be capable of clear thought and reasoned actions. He therefore has to accept responsibility for his own conduct, as it affects him and those around him.

Legally, the employee must 'take reasonable care for the health and safety of himself and of other persons who may be affected by his acts or omissions'. On the other hand, his activities must be properly supervised, and he must be given adequate instruction, training and information, to ensure that he does his job safely. He must, in fact, be controlled and monitored, to ensure that he acts responsibly.

This all indicates the manager's intimate involvement; his own responsibility is entangled with that of his employer, and of the employees to whom he has a duty of care.

We can truly say, then, that responsibility resides in all of us – the Company, its management, its supervisors, its employees. But the manager is the person who makes things happen. And accidents occur only when things happen (or maybe when things which should happen *don't* happen, depending upon how you look at it).

1.2 The Problem Stated

In the light of press reports, television features, union pronouncements, the clutch of fast-breeder safety magazines flooding the market, the statistics hurled at us by a regiment of safety organisations, we must all surely be aware that industry has a health-and-safety problem.

We must know that the problem is a large one, measured by the human yardstick of pain, ill-health, disability, loss of earnings, family distress. It is also an economic problem, measured in terms of plant damage, loss of production, increased insurance costs, legal penalties, impaired industrial relations, and similar loss features.

We know about it – yet the rate of work-related accidents remains alarmingly high.

The annual Report of Her Majesty's Chief Inspector of Factories is a document which records our failure to cope with the hazards of work. The casualty figures which it contains are rather like a battle report, and they exist as an indictment of our way of doing things. They reflect our incompetence, our lack of knowledge, our apparent apathy, our inadequate training provisions, our criminal acceptance of a situation which *can* be improved if we have the will to improve it.

The annual catalogue of maiming, smashing, killing and poisoning indicates our bad management of risks, our casual attitude to safe procedures, our pathetic performance in what should be a field of high endeavour.

Poor safety performance equates with poor management capability, and we who direct the activities of others are, by definition, *managers*. The problem, therefore, is clearly ours.

In numerical terms, the problem is easy to appreciate – very approximately, we kill about 500 people annually, and cause about three-hundred-thousand people to lose time because of work-related injuries. This results in something approaching twenty million man-days lost every year, and it should not be too difficult to imagine the pain, resentment, financial loss and family distress which must be generated.

Published figures, however, do not indicate the huge number of minor injuries which do not result in lost-time and which are therefore not officially reportable. The bumps and bruises, the strains and pains, the cuts and gashes – all the countless minor injuries which are dealt with by the Company nurse or the first-aider or maybe the colleague on the shop floor – these do not feature in the official statistics.

What is visible, then, is the small but cold tip of a huge and chilling iceberg.

If too many noughts on the printed page tend to blunt the sensitivity, it might be useful to examine one's own place of work – whether large or small – and to digest the monthly accident score which is (or which should be) published by the Safety Officer or by the person delegated to perform this function. Multiply this by twelve and reflect upon the quota of pain which *your* salary machine inflicts upon its human cogs over the period of a year.

Having done this, any manager must be capable of evaluating his own share of the corporate failure to cope.

Harsh words, possibly – but injured people indicate a harsh situation.

1.3 What is an Accident?

The old concept of what constitutes 'an accident' has been abandoned by people, prominent in the field of accident prevention, who began to look further than their noses and were rewarded by seeing things as they really are. Old definitions have been examined and found to be inadequate; these have been discarded, and replaced by something nearer the truth.

It must be said, however, that in some of the less flexible of managerial minds, old concepts are still firmly entrenched – there are people who cling stubbornly to the notion that an accident has something to do with somebody getting hurt; that bloodshed or bruising are essential components; that unless somebody suffers personal and obvious injury, no accident has occurred. This is a virulent misconception, which needs to be immediately and enthusiastically purged from the mind, if we are to make any progress in the field of prevention.

Is it necessary to define what we mean by the word 'accident'? Well – yes, it is, because before anyone can begin to put up any sort of a fight, he must know his enemy. St George had to identify *his* dragon; we, too, must do the same. So let's come to terms with terms.

An accident is an unplanned event, which could result in injury to persons, or in damage to plant and equipment or both.

6   Let's Talk About Accidents

As a simple illustration of this simple definition, imagine a hammer, dropped from the working platform of a scaffold, which narrowly misses the driver of a passing fork-lift truck. This would be – we hope – our 'unplanned event'.

Though the hammer missed, it could quite easily have struck the driver or damaged the truck. There was, therefore, a real *potential* for injury to a person or for damage to equipment – possibly both. The incident meets our definition, and is promptly promoted to the status of 'accident'. The fact that the truck remained unscathed and the driver escaped having a hole in his skull is nothing more than a stroke of good luck.

Imagine two incidents which occur in a busy warehouse building:

(1) In one case, a badly stacked batch of heavy wooden pallets collapses, near the door of the emloyees' locker room. The pallets lie strewn all over the floor, immediately in front of the

'An accident is an unplanned event, which could result in injury to persons, or in damage to plant and equipment, or both'.

door, but since nobody was passing by at the time there was no injury caused. A few pallets were damaged, however, and two of them were sent for repairs, to the adjoining maintenance bay.
(2) An hour or so later a carpenter, in the maintenance bay, is busy repairing the pallets. He misses the head of a two-inch nail, and smashes the top of his thumb to a pulp with a hammer.

In the first case, there existed a significant potential for serious injury, in addition to the actual occurrence of some slight damage to a few pallets. The unfortunate choice of location for making a stack of pallets; the implication that they were poorly stacked, resulting in instability; the weight of the pallets, and the fact that a human body is no real match for a ton of collapsing timber; these factors all add up to the possibility of someone being badly injured or perhaps killed. Appropriate action can be taken by the supervisor, to prevent recurrence – like moving the stack to a safe area, where people and pallets are not in mortal conflict, and making sure that pallets are properly stacked in future.

In the second case, all that may be involved is an error of judgement on the part of the carpenter. Assuming that lighting in the maintenance bay is adequate, that the hammer is in good condition, that the carpenter is not half blind or suffering from a hang-over, there is little remedial action which the supervisor can take. (Telling the carpenter to 'be more careful in future' is a waste of breath – he's learned his lesson the hard way, so let's not add insult to injury!)

When these two accidents are considered in terms of their *potential*, therefore, the investigator should find no difficulty in deciding which is the more important, from the point of view of taking preventive action. The one which caused actual and bloody injury was *potentially* far less serious than the one which, by sheer luck, caused no injury at all.

These rather elementary arguments can be summarised by saying that:

(a) An accident does not have to result in bloodshed.
(b) It is vital to be able to appreciate the *potential* of any accident situation, so that the appropriate degree of importance can be given to corrective measures designed to prevent recurrence.
(c) The manager or supervisor has it within his power to anticipate and to prevent certain types of accidents, simply by looking around his domain with a trained and suspicious eye.

Let us therefore turn our backs on the old, easy, devalued way of seeing accidents as broken arms and cut fingers and lumps on the head. These things are nothing more than injuries – and an injury is simply *one possible result* of an accident.

And accidents, in turn, are the consequence of unplanned (unsafe) acts or unplanned (unsafe) conditions performed or created by *people*.

It is difficult to imagine any spirit of evil residing within a ladder, or a fork-truck, or a hammer, or an unlit stairway, or a cylinder of propane. These are inanimate, unthinking, static objects which do absolutely nothing until they are used or abused by people like ourselves who animate them and give them significance. It is *people* who use tools and equipment, who design plant and install it, who create dangerous activities or ignore unsafe conditions.

We can truly say that *people* cause accidents, by what they do or what they neglect to do – and the activities of people, in a factory or in any other place of work, are controlled by Management.

Shall we go a step further and accept the premise that the person in charge – the Manager or Supervisor – is the person who can contribute most to the prevention of accidents?

Creating a safe place of work must be an ambition shared by everyone at the workplace. But the person who manages others must be the one who leads, supervises, instructs, monitors, corrects, makes decisions, initiates and enforces the necessary controls. He must accept the immediate responsibility for what happens in his own patch.

1.4 What is 'Safety'?

While we're busy examining definitions, let's briefly explore the possibility of finding a better way to express the goal we should all be aiming for.

In the dark ages (not all that long ago!) the term used was 'Safety First', and it proved to be meaningless, or irrelevant, or impossible. Anybody insisting upon 'safety first' wouldn't cross the road because in doing so he might get run over. 'Safety First' means not eating, in case you stab yourself with a fork. 'Safety first' implies that every other consideration is secondary. Which means that profit, economic survival, progress, improved living standards, advancement of technology, and our whole modern way of life must take second place to some concept of absolute safety.

Industry, commerce, sport, recreation, etc. all grind to a halt and a great calm descends upon the world, where nobody moves a muscle.

'*Accident Prevention*' is currently an accepted term, since it expresses a positive goal, a real activity, without implying the absolute and the impracticable. So 'accident prevention' is viable, whilst 'safety first' is not.

The weakness inherent in the term 'accident prevention', however, is that people at all levels in society still cling to the concept that 'accidents' happen only to people. Accidents are *caused* by people, but the consequence of accidents range far beyond the human condition. Perhaps we need something better than 'accident prevention', something more ambitious, more valuable, more in line with what should be the goal of every conscientious manager.

'Accident' is rather limiting, even in terms of the definition offered in the previous section. Managers operate in a world beset by economic pressures, where costs have to be controlled in order to protect profits. Accidental (unplanned) losses are a significant feature of operating costs, and need to be evaluated and controlled.

Loss Prevention, in this context, is a very sound philosophy based on the argument that 'loss' can be associated with a whole range of activities and can be traced back to a number of different causes. Injury, plant damage, interference with production, fire, flood, material wastage, theft, legal penalties, commercial espionage, sabotage, power failure, poor industrial relations, storm damage, inflated or punitive insurance premiums, injury compensation, retraining costs, overtime payments – all these are loss-creating factors; all can be anticipated and measured; all can be prevented or their effects minimised.

The individual manager cannot practice comprehensive loss prevention on his own; he needs the support of his peers and of his Company as a corporate entity. What he can do, however, is to absorb the philosophy and to recognise the losses which can occur in his own neck of the woods which are caused by the multitude of faults, mishaps, miscalculations, hazards, inefficiencies and anomalies which are part of the daily scene.

By accepting the true definition of the word 'accident' he will have travelled the first few vital steps along the road to Accident Prevention. By thinking in terms of the *losses* involved, he'll have taken a few important strides further. All that now remains is for him to recognise that a major part of his job is to control and minimise any losses which his Company may suffer – as part of the perfectly legitimate business activity of making a lawful profit –

and what was once called 'Safety First' emerges as the more logical and practical endeavour which we now call 'Loss Prevention'.

The maintenance of health and safety at the workplace is simply a very important detail on the broad canvas of Loss Prevention.

1.5 The Cost of Injuries

Let's look, for a moment, at the cost of those injuries which result from accidents.

There is a school of thought – attended in the main by shop stewards and others, who don't have responsibility for budget control or the need to understand a balance sheet – which says that 'safety' has nothing to do with cost. The theory is that one cannot measure the cost of human suffering, therefore no employer should put a price upon it, nor consider the cost of preventing it.

This is a false premise, and patently absurd, since it takes no account of a very practical need – that of balancing the risk (and the consequences) of an accident on one side of the scale, against the cost of eliminating the risk on the other side of the scale. Risk, consequences and cost of prevention are relative. There are certain people who consider that the 'cost' of giving up mountaineering is greater than the 'cost' of falling off and getting killed. This must necessarily be a very personal choice, and has nothing to do with the employer/employee relationship, since the mountaineer has no contract with the mountain. But it does illustrate the point that a value-judgement is necessary, even in cases of such extreme consequence.

Bringing the argument closer to home, however, it is obvious that no Company would consider an outlay of ten thousand pounds in order to eliminate the risk of Fred getting a splinter in his finger from the sweeping brush handle. Nor would any Company refuse to supply an adequate machine guard for a powered guillotine which threatens to drag Fred into its jaws and mince him to a pulp. Value-judgements have to be made.

On his own patch the manager is constantly faced with such judgements, since in most places there is a steady procession of new situations, new equipment, new procedures, new risks and (not the least consideration) new attitudes to risk acceptance, by the enforcement authorities and by the workforce. Management therefore has the task of evaluating risks and consequences, and deciding what prevention measures to take, at what cost, and with what degree of priority.

To do this intelligently, he must have some insight into the cost of injuries – not only the financial cost, but what we might term the social cost, also. This might best be expressed in terms of cost to the Victim, the Company, and the Nation.

Cost to the Victim. The employee's capital asset is invested in his ability to attend and perform, at his place of work. Take that away from him, and his losses begin to accumulate quickly. His costs are very personal ones, and because he's at the sharp end of the incident he will naturally feel his position very strongly. The victim's costs are by no means exclusively financial. They might well include:

Pain and suffering.
Loss of wages.
Loss of overtime.
Loss of promotion prospects.
Curtailment of leisure activities.
Long-term disablement.
Loss of social intercourse.
Psychological damage.
Family distress.
And perhaps the ultimate cost – death.

It would not strain the imagination unduly to add a few more items to this list. Use, as a model, the skilled machinist who may be on a production bonus, with prospects of promotion to a supervisory grade if he gets through his interview next week. He has a strikingly good-looking wife, a wide circle of friends with whom he enjoys a hectic social round, he plays squash like a demon and his two kids think he's wonderful. Breaking his ankle by falling over that silly duckboard with a hole in it, alongside his mate's workbench, has made a dramatic difference to his life during the next few weeks. Pity somebody else got the supervisory grade; shame about the ankle – let's hope it doesn't have any lasting effect on his squash prowess; they say his daughter cried all night, when they brought him home in plaster up to his knee; never mind – it was just a pure accident, and he'll get money 'on the sick', won't he?

Cost to the Company. The Company will suffer a different range of costs, possibly including:

Lost production.
Damage to equipment.
Repair and replacement cost.

Consequential overtime costs.
Increased insurance premiums.
Legal penalties.
Compensation expenses.
Cost of investigation and documentation.
Industrial relations problems.
Loss of goodwill and reputation.

There is also a variety of 'hidden costs', which the Company doesn't need and can't really afford. Remember that we're talking about 'accidents' by definition, not just injuries. There are many other cost factors which can be sensibly added to this list, and they must all appear on the debit side of the Company's balance sheet. So really, no employer can afford, or ignore the cost of, accidents and injuries. To take a lax view of a poor safety record is, among other follies, just plain bad management.

Cost to the Nation. The Company may be seen as a microcosm of the Nation, when considering costs. The nation, therefore, as a collection of Companies and individuals, suffers the accrued expense of production losses associated with injury and damage accidents, National Health and medical costs, and all the financial drain of industrial accident and sickness benefits paid to victims.

Cost to the individual Manager. This is a factor which the man in the driving seat will have to determine for himself. It might well involve the nagging little question, 'Could I have prevented its happening –?

Accidents, injuries, job-related illness, therefore, impose cost burdens which we all have to bear, directly or indirectly, and which are unnecessary and, in the main, preventable.

The manager is right in the front line of the battle to cut costs; it's part of his job to operate his department efficiently and economically. Accidents represent failure and waste.

1.6 Recording Accidents

In order to monitor the progress made in accident prevention (or maybe the lack of progress!) it is obviously necessary to keep records. How this is done will vary considerably, depending upon the size of the Company, the type and quantity of information demanded by management and unions, the facilities available for producing and displaying such records, the nature of the business and of the types of accidents which occur at the workplace, etc.

There are various ways of expressing safety performance; in general, the method chosen must fit the circumstances of the particular employer. Basically, however, management and workforce need to know:

(a) The number of accidents occurring during each month and each year, in relation to the total number of employees at risk during the period under examination.
(b) How the current period compares with past periods, so that trends and long-term performance can be observed.
(c) The types of accidents which are occurring, and where they occur.

In very small Companies with a very stable workforce, a crude numerical total of accidents per month may satisfy the uncritical reader. This sort of presentation is extremely basic and not particularly informative. It doesn't tell us, for instance, how many people were exposed to risk during the period, or for how long they were exposed. Let's therefore look at some better ways of assessing our performance.

Frequency Rate is a traditional measurement for 'lost-time' accidents. It can be calculated for any stated period – monthly, annually, etc. – by applying a simple arithmetic formula.

Lost-Time Frequency Rate is the number of lost-time accidents multiplied by 100 000, divided by the number of man-hours worked during the period under review.

Looking only at lost-time accidents, however, is not the fairest way of presenting the picture. In many cases lost-time has limited relevance to the severity of an injury. Some employees are prone to lose time for quite trivial reasons; others are more inclined to soldier on with a bad back or a bandaged wrist until the weekend, or until the pain goes away! The difference in attitude between two employees can make a large difference in a month's Frequency Rate.

Incidence Rate is a better indicator, since it takes account of *all* injuries sustained in a particular period, whether causing lost-time or not, and it relates to the total workforce. Incidence Rate is the number of job-related injuries recorded in any one period multiplied by 100, divided by the average number of people employed during the period under review.

The primary weakness in this system, however, is that some of the quite trivial injuries may not be reported by the employee involved – which raises the point that immediate reporting of *all* accidents must be insisted upon by management, if a true indication of safety performance is to be achieved.

14 Let's Talk About Accidents

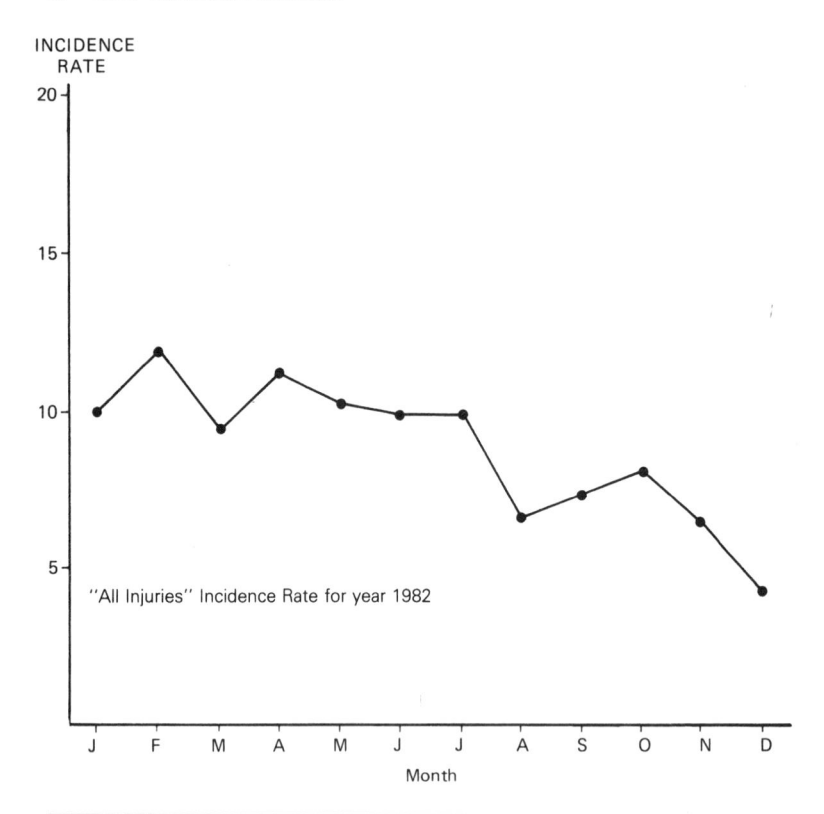

INCIDENCE RATE

"All Injuries" Incidence Rate for year 1982

Month	Injuries	Workforce	I.R.
Jan.	15	150	10.0
Feb	18	150	12.0
Mar	14	148	9.5
Apr	16	142	11.3
May	15	146	10.3
June	14	140	10.0
July	12	120	10.0
Aug	8	120	6.7
Sept	9	120	7.5
Oct	10	123	8.1
Nov	8	123	6.5
Dec	5	120	4.2

'Incidence Rate' is the number of injuries in any one month multiplied by 100, divided by the average number of people employed during that month.

Monthly Incidence Rate

INCIDENCE RATE

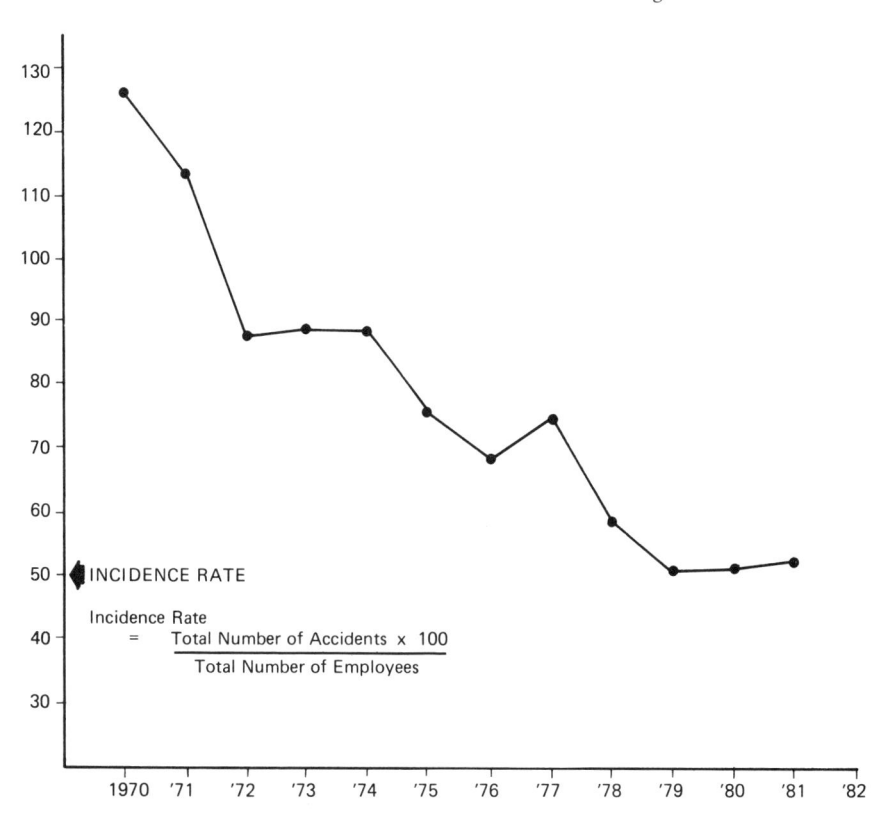

Incidence Rate = $\dfrac{\text{Total Number of Accidents} \times 100}{\text{Total Number of Employees}}$

Year	Accidents	Workforce	Inc. Rate
1970	1687	1134	126
1971	1479	1305	113
1972	1112	1271	87.5
1973	1144	1284	89.1
1974	1140	1288	88.5
1975	967	1281	75.25
1976	879	1269	68.6
1977	965	1286	75
1978	668	1130	59.1
1979	536	1111	50.6
1980	574	1104	52
1981	505	955	52.8

Annual Incidence Rate

Presentation of accident statistics can be as basic or as ornamental as the Company sees fit to make them – bearing in mind that a simple chart says a lot more than just a page of numbers. Some graph paper, a pot of glue and a pair of scissors, plus access to a photocopier, are the main requirements.

To indicate short term and long term trends, charts showing monthly results *and* annual results are essential. Comparing current performance with past performance can generate a glow of quiet satisfaction, or can trigger-off some intense corrective activity, depending upon the direction taken by that meandering black line on the chart. Circulation of the statistics will depend upon available facilities. A notice board reserved for health and safety information is the basic minimum. A notice board in each section/department is better, together with photocopies to all management staff and safety representatives/safety committee members. The aim should be to inform and involve as many people as possible. Co-operation will depend upon good communication.

So much for totals, but what about the nature of the accidents which occur? It is essential to know what sorts of accidents are being recorded, and where they are happening.

Again, much will depend upon the size and nature of the Company, and the diversity of departments or workplaces within the premises. A small joinery on one floor, with an office in the corner, would not merit an elaborate presentation. But if there are workshops, laboratories, production lines, warehouses, offices, stores and other departments within the curtilage of a factory, then something more detailed is in order.

A useful system of presenting additional information is to list the various departments within the factory premises and to show the number of accidents, according to classification, which have occurred in each department over a particular period.

This given each manager or supervisor an opportunity to see the pattern of accidents in his own area of responsibility and to focus his attention on any particular problem which emerges.

Classification of accidents should not follow a rigid formula – the list of headings should be tailored to suit the needs of the Company. A suitably designed Classification Chart can provide quite an interesting picture of life in various sections of the undertaking, as the following (admittedly exaggerated) example suggests.

A quick glance at the figures for the month should convince the Workshop Supervisor that the sun has stopped shining over his

Table 1.1 Work-related accidents: classification chart   Month – June 1982

Classification	Work shop	Press shop	Test lab.	Stores	Office block	Other areas	This month	Last month	Totals This year	Last year
Gas/fume							–	–	2	3
Burns/scalds							–	1	3	5
Machinery							–	–	–	–
Eyes (dust only)						2	2	1	–	18
Eyes (other foreign bodies)	1	1	2	1		3	8	5	30	50
Persons falling	3						3	2	15	30
Falling objects	3						3	2	13	28
Stepping on	2						2	1	14	24
Striking against	2						2	2	10	20
Manual handling		1		3			1	2	3	8
Transport	2						5	4	23	40
Handling tools	4						4	4	20	40
Handling materials		1					1	1	5	13
Handling equipment			1				1	2	7	13
Rashes							–	–	4	3
Unclassified				1		4	5	2	30	46

Workforce	36	25	5	18	19	32

Totals

	Work shop	Press shop	Test lab.	Stores	Office block	Other areas
This month	17	3	3	5	–	9
Last month	12	2	2	4	1	8
This year	80	15	18	22	3	48
Last year	144	20	33	50	8	86

37	29	186	341

own particular patch, that he's running an untidy shop (since people seem to be falling about, stepping on things which hurt their feet, being struck by objects dropping off benches, etc.), and that he has a serious problem with fork-trucks coming into the shop. He also has a workforce of careless people, since they appear to injure themselves with their tools – or are the hammers all rounded, the spanners all gaping, the chisel-heads all burred and the files all bereft of handles? He's had 17 accidents in his section and the Works Manager should be climbing up the wall, closely followed by the union-appointed safety representative.

The figures for the Stores also point to 'transport' accidents. Perhaps the fork-trucks are driven by the same group of drivers who charge blindly around the workshop. Or are traffic and demarcation lines not a feature of the Company's safety codes? Maybe people can't hear the trucks coming, because of background noise – or is driver-training a bit sketchy, to the point of being non-existent?

Eye injuries are fairly evenly spread over all sections. Perhaps people need educating or supervising (or both) with regard to wearing eye protection? Maybe there isn't any eye protection; or maybe what's on offer is not suitable for the risks encountered?

Alright – this is a very superficial analysis of an imaginary set of statistics in a fictitious factory. But it does illustrate the possibilities

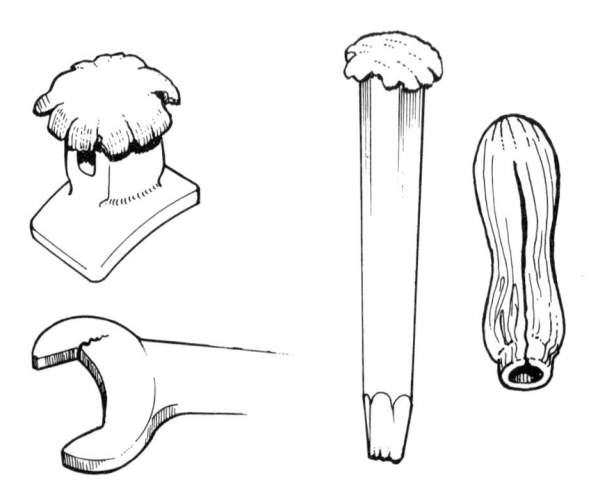

'. . . or are the hammers all rounded, the spanners all gaping, the chisel-heads all burred and the files all bereft of handles . . .?'

presented by a monthly breakdown of accidents by area and classification. Knowledge is power, in the struggle to stop people hurting each other!

1.7 Accident Investigation

There's an old adage which exhorts us to 'never waste an accident'. This simply means that *every* accident – no matter how trivial it may appear to be – should be properly investigated, since we can always learn something from the investigation. We must never prejudge; never jump to conclusions; never make assumptions without carrying out checks.

Even in the case of a very minor incident, a visit to the scene and a chat with the victim, and with any available witness, will usually reveal something of interest, something which will point the way to action which can be taken to prevent recurrence. And it is this factor which becomes important, once the event has taken place – a means of preventing recurrence is all that can be salvaged from an otherwise totally bad situation.

During an investigation of any accident, whether major or minor, the two main elements to be looked for are the unsafe acts and the unsafe conditions which were the basic cause of the accident.

Unsafe acts (involving people) can take any number of forms – using equipment incorrectly or without authority, defeating safety devices for reasons of convenience, failure to use protective clothing or equipment, ignoring routine safety instructions or safe working methods, indulging in horseplay or carelessness, undertaking jobs which are beyond one's capability or training – the list can be extended to include a whole raft of follies and misguided actions.

Unsafe conditions (again involving people) can also include a catholic assortment of triggers – unguarded machinery, bad design or construction of equipment, inadequate maintenance, unsafe working procedures, insufficient training or instruction, untidy place of work, defective tools, inadequate lighting, lack of supervision, ineffective protective clothing or equipment, obstructed or unsafe means of access – and many other factors which constitute traps for the unwary victim.

20   Let's Talk About Accidents

The scale of the consequences will often match the enormity of the unsafe act or the unsafe condition, but not always. There can be accidents in which little mistakes cause horrendous end-results; there are others in which serious lapses or grossly illegal actions lead to only minor mishaps – it's very much a matter of luck, either way.

The true story of a very senior manager who inspected a very large vessel containing an explosive mixture of gases is a case in

'. . . the consequences of an accident are not always predictable . . .'

point. He looked into an open inspection manhole, with his pipe still in his mouth. The resulting blast left him with singed eyebrows, a ringing noise in his ears, and the last inch of expensive pipe-stem still clamped between his teeth. What turned out to be a rather comic episode could have resulted in his going into orbit via a hole in the roof, instead. It just illustrates the fact that consequences are not always predictable.

Investigation, then, must be an exercise in identifying the *unsafe acts* and the *unsafe conditions* which comprise the *cause* of an accident. We are not interested in conclusions which point to bad luck, or acts of God, or similar flights of fancy.

There are one or two further points to be made about accident investigation. Perhaps the most important one is that its purpose is to discover the true cause, so that action can be taken which will prevent a recurrence. It must be strongly emphasised that the purpose is *not* to apportion blame, or to point an accusing finger at any individual person who might be involved. An investigation which assumes the characteristics of an inquisition will put the kiss of death on the whole procedure – people will adopt defensive attitudes, will withhold possibly vital information, will rationalise their own actions and involvement, will even lie and distort the facts, if they think that they or their mates will be accused of causing the accident. The purpose of the investigation, therefore, must be made perfectly clear at the outset, whether it involves a formal and far-ranging inquiry or just a brief chat to Fred at the scene of the incident.

Where an investigation is carried out by an appointed team – possibly including a mix of management and union people – then there can be a concealed but nevertheless potent conflict of interests. Management members will wish to arrive at the facts and identify the true cause, but there might also be an unconscious desire to minimise any hint of 'blame' attaching to the Company. Union people, quite naturally, will wish to find the true cause but will also have one eye firmly focused on the Company's liability in the matter, so that the goose can be made to lay a golden egg of compensation for the injured brother. These are inescapable impediments to arriving at the whole truth, particularly in the case of moderately serious 'injury-type' accidents, and the facts need to be faced.

Another feature which presents difficulty, in some cases, is the intrusion of *opinion*, where only facts are needed. Commentators present opinion with such an air of certainty that the investigator can easily be misled into accepting it as real evidence.

Another actual case illustrates this. The plumber whose ladder slipped whilst he was coming down from a platform was taken to the Medical Department and the ladder was left lying undisturbed on the asphalt floor until a prompt investigation could be mounted. The thing was part of an extension ladder, and had wheels at one end. Two 'witnesses' (who weren't really witnesses, since they had their backs to the incident and were some distance away) stated with complete conviction that the ladder was used with the wheels on the floor, so 'it must have slid away on its wheels whilst he was coming down'. This seemed a perfectly obvious and acceptable explanation – except that the position of the ladder on the floor, where it had been left, plus the marks on the floor made by the ends of the ladder styles, plus the completely dry and clean condition of the wheels, plus the later evidence of the mate who had placed the ladder in position for the plumber, all showed that the ladder had been used correctly, and not with the 'wheels-end' down. It had simply slipped, on a very wet and greasy asphalt floor. Opinion can be convenient and cosy, but *evidence* must be based upon fact.

Additionally, in any investigation of any importance, real evidence collected as soon as possible after the event, preferably in the company of an observer, can be of vital importance at a later date. Measurements, diagrams, notes, even photographs, are most essential. They benefit the victim and the Company, since they can resolve disputes and arguments which tend to develop subsequently. There is nothing sinister about collecting such evidence in a permanent form, even though the camera is sometimes seen as a Company or a union weapon in a possible clash of interests. It simply records the truth – and this is a commodity which hurts nobody.

Finally, the question of who should carry out an investigation emerges. Is it the supervisor in isolation, or the supervisor plus the shop steward, or the section manager, or a sprinkling of other interested parties, or the Safety Officer, or . . .?

Obviously, there can be no fixed rule for this, since there are several factors which impinge upon the question. Investigation procedure will depend upon the seriousness of the accident, the size of the Company, the facilities which are available, the staff structure and the style of management which obtains in the Company.

Large scale concerns will have a Safety Officer in post, who is able to enlist the help of technical experts and mount a comprehensive and wide-ranging investigation of a serious accident.

Where the incident is heavy with potential or attended by significant injury or plant damage the location head of such a Company might initiate a full enquiry, involving senior technical staff, and demand a full report containing conclusions and recommendations. Smaller companies will need to do the best they can with the limited resources available. Where a serious accident occurs, however, the top man on site should surely be involved in the investigation, and his appointed team must be equally concerned with seeking the cause and the remedy.

Less serious events must obviously be investigated by the supervisor, as a matter of routine responsibility. He is the person in charge, the person who knows the score, the person who can take action to prevent recurrence. He is the person, too, who must decide whether or not to call in the Safety Officer or his own manager, when the need becomes apparent.

The important thing is that the investigation is conducted, *every time*, and that it bears fruit. 'Never waste an accident'.

1.8 Reporting Accidents

Depending upon the size of the Company, and the safety procedures which it operates, there may or may not be an Accident Report Form in use. Most Companies of any appreciable size use accident report forms of some sort – the style of the form will vary, from place to place, and its value and comprehensiveness will also vary according to the emphasis which an employer places upon accident prevention.

There is no single 'best' type of accident report form; each one should be designed to suit the needs of the individual Company in which it is used. The design of the form, and the procedure for using it, will be matters for management to decide, after taking advice from its Safety Officer.

The value of a *properly completed* accident report form is that it:

(a) records the full circumstances of an accident, so that the facts may be retrieved from the files at a future date, in the event of subsequent compensation claims or other eventualities;
(b) provides the supervisor or manager with an opportunity to record his recommendations for prevention of recurrence;
(c) may be used by the Safety Officer or some other members of management as a source of statistics, the identification of trends, the design of aditional accident prevention procedures, etc.

| SAFETY | | | | | Ref. No. | 14 |

ACCIDENT REPORT

| Name | BLOGGS, F. | No. | 1 2 8 2 | Plant/Section | FURNACES | P R O D U C T I O N |

| Usual Assignment | CHARGE HAND | Assignment at time | NORMAL |

| Date reported | 18.12.80 | Time | 14-20 | Date of accident | Day 18 | Month 12 | Year 80 | Time | 14.10 |

Details:— Injury to left hand---states charging door of Furnace dropped, and rabbling rod struck his hand.

H. Morgan, S.R.N.

Supervisor's Report. (Return to Safety & Fire Officer, on completion.)

Describe what happened. He was rabbling No.2 Furnace. The charging door suspension chain snapped, and the door dropped onto the rabbler. The rabbler handle "kicked", and jammed his hand against the door support stanchion.

What do you think was the basic cause? Weakness in suspension chain. Examination showed stretching of links, and broken link had worn very thin.

(Chains on both furnaces have now been renewed).

Name any witnesses. 376 - P. Cartwright.

Action to prevent recurrence? 3-monthly examination of door suspension chains, by Plant Engineer, with record of examinations kept in Section Log Book. Renewal of chains on basis of Engineer's recommendation.

Action initiated? Yes - from 20/12/80 Or recommended? Date 19/12/80

Signed (Supervisor) K. Blightworthy. Signed (Manager/Engineer) M. Williston.

Accident Report Form (page 1)

SAFETY				Ref. No.	014

ACCIDENT REPORT

Name	BLOGGS, F.	No.	1 2 8 2	Plant/Section	FURNACES	P R O D U C T I O N

Usual Assignment	CHARGE HAND	Assignment at time	NORMAL

Date reported	18.12.80	Time	14.20	Date of accident	Day 18	Month 12	Year 80	Time	14.10

Details:— Inury to left hand---states charging door of Furnace dropped, and rabbling rod struck his hand.

H. Morgan, S.R.N.

Treatment:— Severe bruising outer aspect left hand. No bleeding. Hand washed, C.W. soaked, L/T cream applied, and dry bandage. To return for further treatment, end of shift. Supervisor informed.

			29 30	31	
Lost Time	L T	R V	X	From 20.12.80

			32 33	34		35	36	37	38	39	40
Gas/Fume	G F	R V		L/R	Code	L/R	Code	L/R	Code
Burns/Scalds	B S	R V		L	H				
Machinery	M C	R V							
Eyes (Dust)	E D	R V		Codes					
Eyes (Other)	E O	R V		Head	T				
Persons Falling	P F	R V		Eyes	E				
Falling Objects	F O	R V		Neck	N				
Stepping On	S O	R V		Shoulder	S				
Striking Against	S A	R V		Abdomen	X				
Manual Handling	M H	R V		Chest	C				
Transport	T R	R V		Back	B				
Handling Tools	H T	R V	X	Arm	A				
Handling Materials	H M	R V		Hand	H	✓			
Handling Equipment	H E	R V		Leg	L				
Rashes	R A	R V		Foot	F				
Unclassified	U C	R V		Other	O				

Accident Report Form (page 2)

The example of an Accident Report Form is not presented as the best or the most useful – it simply illustrates the type of report which might be used in a medium-size undertaking where there happens to be a first-aid department and a person who carries out the duties of Safety Officer.

Ideally pads of printed self-copying forms should be kept at the first-aid room. The first part of the report would be completed by the attendant on duty, who would take details from the injured employee. This top copy should then be handed to the patient who, on returning to his job after treatment, would report back to his supervisor. (Should the employee be unable to return to his place of work after treatment, the first-aid attendant would have to inform the supervisor and pass the top copy to him by some other means.)

Upon receiving the top copy, the supervisor will be required to complete his part of the Report – preferably in the presence of the employee, and after investigation of the accident. Having made his recommendations he will pass it on to his manager for information and for any further comment. The completed Report is then forwarded to the Safety Officer.

After disposing of the top copy, the first-aid attendant would enter treatment details on the lower half of the second page, and this remains in the pad as a permanent record.

The value of this format is that the supervisor cannot remain unaware of the accident and is obliged to pass investigation details through his manager to the Safety Officer. The latter, in turn, is equally certain to be made aware of the accident and of the action or recommendations for preventing recurrence.

It must be said, however, that the 'investigation' report from the supervisor is only as good as the person who completes the details – a conscientious and responsible supervisor can contribute greatly to accident prevention by carrying out a proper investigation, taking the necessary action, and recording all the relevant facts on the report form.

It must also be said that in many cases there may be little or no remedial action to take, and little or no comment to make – the brief description on the top part of the first page may have said it all. In this event, 'as above' could be an appropriate acknowledgement that the form has passed through a supervisor's hands. Before writing 'as above', however, the supervisor should be very certain that he's not 'wasting an accident'.

The reporting procedure does not end there, however, since there is a statutory requirement to report certain classes of accidents to the Health and Safety Executive.

This requirement was, for a while, enshrined in the 'Notification of Accidents and Dangerous Occurrencies Regulations, 1980' (Statutory Instrument 1980, No. 804, obtainable from HMSO).

The complete set of Regulations ran to fourteen pages, and contained the usual full measure of self-indulgent obscurity and officialese beloved of the civil service poets' laureate. A much better investment was the Health and Safety Series Booklet, serial number HS(R)5, published by the Health & Safety Executive. This excellent publication contained clear and readable instructions on how to comply with the legal requirements, together with appendices and notes on record keeping.

Unfortunately, however, with effect from 5th April 1983 payment by the DHSS of industrial injuries benefit was abandoned and this effectively destroyed the sense of the 1980 Regulations. At the present time, therefore, only a part of these Regulations remains in force, and we await the emergence of updated reporting requirement from the H. & S. Executive.

That part which remains is, very briefly, as follows:

1. Accidents resulting in death or major injury, or incidents defined as 'dangerous occurrences', must be notified to the local office of the enforcing authority by telephone as soon as reasonably practicable. This notification must be confirmed in writing, on Form F2508, within seven days. A copy of F2508 must be kept for record purposes, and must be made available to the enforcing authority or the appointed safety representative for inspection, if so required. Definition of 'major injury' and 'dangerous occurrences' are contained in the Regulations and in the Booklet.
2. Additionally, records must be kept of all accidents which result in loss of work for three days or more.
3. Industrial disablement or sickness claim forms relating to employees must be completed and returned to the DHSS upon their request. A copy of the completed form will then be forwarded by the DHSS to the Health and Safety Executive.

For record keeping purposes, the employer should use Part 1 of the official General Register, (F2509), obtainable from HMSO, or he may prepare his own register – provided that it contains the same information, which includes:

(a) The date of the accident or the dangerous occurrence.
(b) Location of the accident or the dangerous occurrence.
(c) A brief description of the circumstances.

28 Let's Talk About Accidents

(d) Where injury has occurred, details of the person injured – name, sex, age, occupation and nature of injury.

Proper reporting and recording procedures are very important features of any Company's health and safety responsibility. It must also be appreciated that detailed reports can be very useful in the event of claims for compensation against the Company by employees who suffer injury at work. In such cases the Company's Insurers will need a full account of the circumstances, with names of witnesses and other vital information. Investigation, reporting and recording are essential management activities which in the long term are undeniably cost-effective.

1.9 Safety Inspections

The best time to study accidents, of course, is before they happen. This is the essence of safety inspections – to seek out the unsafe conditions, to uncover the unsafe actions, *before* they become accident causes.

This is not as trite as it may sound, since a programme of routine inspections, undertaken by people who know what to look for, followed by an inspection report and prompt action to correct the reported faults, has proved beyond any shadow of doubt to have had a dramatic effect on safety performance.

There is nothing new about the philosophy of safety inspections. What is recent, perhaps, is the jargon which has been adopted to describe various styles of inspection. Let's just briefly discuss the different packages on offer, before dealing with the type of inspection commonly in use.

Safety Audit. This is a very wide-ranging exercise, in which many areas of a Company's activity are examined in depth. The objective is to identify those areas of weakness or imperfection in the Company's operations which can lead to accidents and loss-making situations. The audit team will spend as much time as it takes, and will look very closely into such areas as plant design; plant layout and construction; safety training and job training quality; safety policy; operating procedures; the attitude to safety of management, supervisors and employees; the quality of management staff; fire prevention procedures; planning for major emergencies – in fact, any number of aspects which have a bearing on accidental loss.

It may be interesting to note that the Health and Safety Executive is now requiring its Inspectors to interest themselves in the Safety Audit type of inspection. These experienced, erudite, but sadly overworked gentlemen (and ladies, or course) are still casting a beady eye on poor standards of machine guarding, holes in the floor, broken ladders, etc. But they are also delving deep into the Company's attitudes, resources, technical ability, training activities and working procedures.

Safety Survey. This is a much more sharply focussed examination; a hard look at an area which has a known problem. It could result from a safety audit, where a particular weakness has been discovered; it could be an in-depth analysis of an individual operating procedure, or some aspect of a single plant or activity. The objective is to identify the fly in the ointment, catch it, and kill it dead.

Safety Tour. This is merely an unscheduled inspection of a work area, to check on such items as good housekeeping, general safety standards, obvious hazards – a sort of impromptu critical walkabout. It has its value, in that it keeps people on their toes.

Safety Sampling. This is a procedure in which a team of trained observers carries out a regular tour of the work area, armed with a pad and pencil. They usually follow the same route, spending about half an hour once every week, noting all the faults and defects along the way. The total score of faults – not weighted to reflect risk severity – is compared with last week's total, simply to gain an impression of the trend in performance or conditions. (What happens in those areas which are not on the prescribed route is anybody's guess.) This could be a useful exercise if the whole plant or premises could be sub-divided into safety sampling routes, with each route assigned to a team of samplers. It could be of benefit in a continuous-shift-work undertaking, where at least five supervisors are based in one plant or section. Each supervisor could 'safety-sample' his own prescribed part of the plant for a period, after which the areas could be rotated so that supervisors take over a new area for a while.

Scheduled Safety Inspection. This is the routine, disciplined, solid, no-nonsense technique which turns over the stones to reveal the unsafe acts and conditions lurking beneath. How it is done will depend upon the size of the Company, the agreed management/union inspection procedures, the number of sections into which the undertaking can be sub-divided, the time off-the-job which is available to the personnel involved, and similar factors.

Ideally, the premises should be divided into a convenient number of sections, with an inspection team assigned to each section. A co-ordinator – normally the Safety Officer – should be given the task of scheduling the routine inspection of each section on a regular basis, and he would accompany each team during each inspection.

The inspection teams *must* be kept small – a horde of people trampling through the section, splitting off into corners and by-ways, stopping to chat with mates, reporting faults which nobody else has seen and calling the other members back to have a look, straying, getting lost and having to be searched for – this sort of circus is frustrating and time-consuming and gives safety a bad name.

Experience indicates that four people comprise an adequate team – the section supervisor, the Safety Officer, and two union-appointed safety representatives. (One safety rep. would be even better, but where there may be production and craft unions in the same section, protocol must be observed.)

The team should meet at an appointed time – on the dot – and make as complete a tour of the section as time allows, sticking together, agreeing the hazards they've spotted, giving each one a 'hazard rating', and not wasting time on issues which are unrelated to their stated objective, which is the discovery of potential accident causes.

After the inspection – on the same day, preferably – the Safety Officer should prepare the Inspection Report and pass copies to all interested parties. This report should include a list of all the faults discovered, with a rating letter (e.g. A, B, or C) against each one, denoting its hazard potential and the degree of priority which should be given to remedial action. The report should be sent to the section manager, the supervisor, the engineer responsible for maintenance, the members of the inspection team, and any other members of the safety committee which serves the section.

The team will be looking, during the inspection, for physical, chemical, procedural and environmental faults on the section – unsafe acts as well as unsafe conditions.

The value of this type of exercise is that it provides for a joint approach to the discovery of accident causes, it becomes a regular feature of the accident prevention programme within the section, it ensures that the supervisor is deeply involved in running a safe section, and it introduces people who can periodically see things with a fresh eye. (It's suprising how often a person can walk past an obvious hazard on his own patch and not notice it – perhaps the total picture is so familiar to him that he can't see the wood for the trees. This is not a condemnation; it's quite understandable and human.)

Inspections, then, are an integral part of loss prevention, and the supervisor/manager is an integral part of the inspection team.

The foregoing description of a safety inspection might send cold shivers down the spine of a hard-pressed manager struggling to run a small business with minimal staff and a few dozen employees. (Where's the Safety Officer? Who's got safety representatives to spare? What 'engineer in charge of maintenance'? My business isn't big enough to chop into sections for inspection teams to crawl all over the . . .)

Yes – this is appreciated. But the concept of a safety inspection is sound, and the procedure can be adapted and modified and wrung out until it fits the size and resources of the business. The whole idea is simply to cast a critical eye over the workplace, its hardware, its working methods, its general condition – and to discover the hazards *before* they bite the unwary employee.

Part 2
The Legal Aspects

2.1 Health and Safety Legislation

Health and safety law never stands still. There are minor modifications (and some major ones) taking place constantly, as new regulations and codes emerge to cope with new technology, new social attitudes and new standards of safety.

Our responsibilities under the law are unequivocal and inescapable, in this land of the free, and who would have it otherwise! Safety law is usually generated in response to our realisation of fresh hazards (or our belated discovery of old ones – e.g. asbestos) and, though some employers justly complain about the sheer volume of restrictive statutes, we must remember that history has shown the need for regulation of the way we conduct ourselves.

Safety legislation did not suddenly spring into life in its present form. It was born, a very puny baby, out of the horrors of the Industrial Revolution. In the harsh dawn of the 19th century, when adults and children worked an eighty-four-hour week, conditions in factory premises were cruelly bad. Illness, deformity, injury and pain were woven shamelessly into the fabric of life, and fever epidemics among workers in the ill-ventilated and dirty factories were commonplace. Without restrictive legislation, fear and indifference were partners in the crime of exploitation.

The growth of safety legislation in the United Kingdom is a fascinating study of the gradual awakening of a nation's collective conscience.

It will not be necessary to enter into a detailed description of the process in these pages, though the story is not without its share of pathos and romance. For those who have a feeling for social history, a short booklet entitled *The History of Work Safety Legislation*, published by RoSPA, contains the essential story (Publication No. IS/108 from RoSPA, Cannon House, The Priory Queensway, Birmingham).

For our purpose, however, we shall look only at the current situation – though not in exhaustive detail. To produce anything like a comprehensive review of extant health and safety legislation would require a major effort of research and production, resulting in a book of massive proportions, daunting complexity and blinding small print. This book is not in that league.

What can be offered, however, is an introduction to the more basic Acts and their associated Regulations, so that operating managers and others can gain some insight into what the law expects of employers and employees.

There are certain fundamental items of safety legislation – the primary Acts – which become required reading for the conscientious manager. He must obtain copies, read them carefully, and keep them readily available for reference. Without them, and without the various Regulations which apply to his own Company's operations, he could be forced to rely upon hearsay or the often inaccurate interpretations peddled by half-trained safety representatives, or the occasional gem of wisdom passed on by the Safety Officer – if the Company happens to have one.

The appendices to this book include lists of those items which constitute essential reading, plus other titles which are desirable and useful volumes to have on the office bookshelf.

As employers, or representatives of the employer, we are mainly concerned with two aspects of the law relating to health and safety at the workplace. These are common law and statute law.

2.1.1 Common Law

This is a civil law of redress which in the occupational field is mainly used by an employee to make a claim for compensation from his employer, in respect of a job-related injury or illness suffered at work due to alleged negligence on the part of the employer.

Claims in common law have become more numerous over the past decade or so, due to the awakened interest of trade unions who initiate them on behalf of their members. Employers are required by law to hold an Employers' Liability insurance policy in order to ensure that, should an injury claim against the employer be upheld, the employee is guaranteed the compensation awarded by the court.

The Employers' Liability Insurance Certificate must be displayed in a prominent place, so that the Company's employees are able to see it.

It follows that the Insurance Company's scale of premiums will partly reflect the claims history of the employers whom they insure

Fire Precautions Act 1971
CHAPTER 40

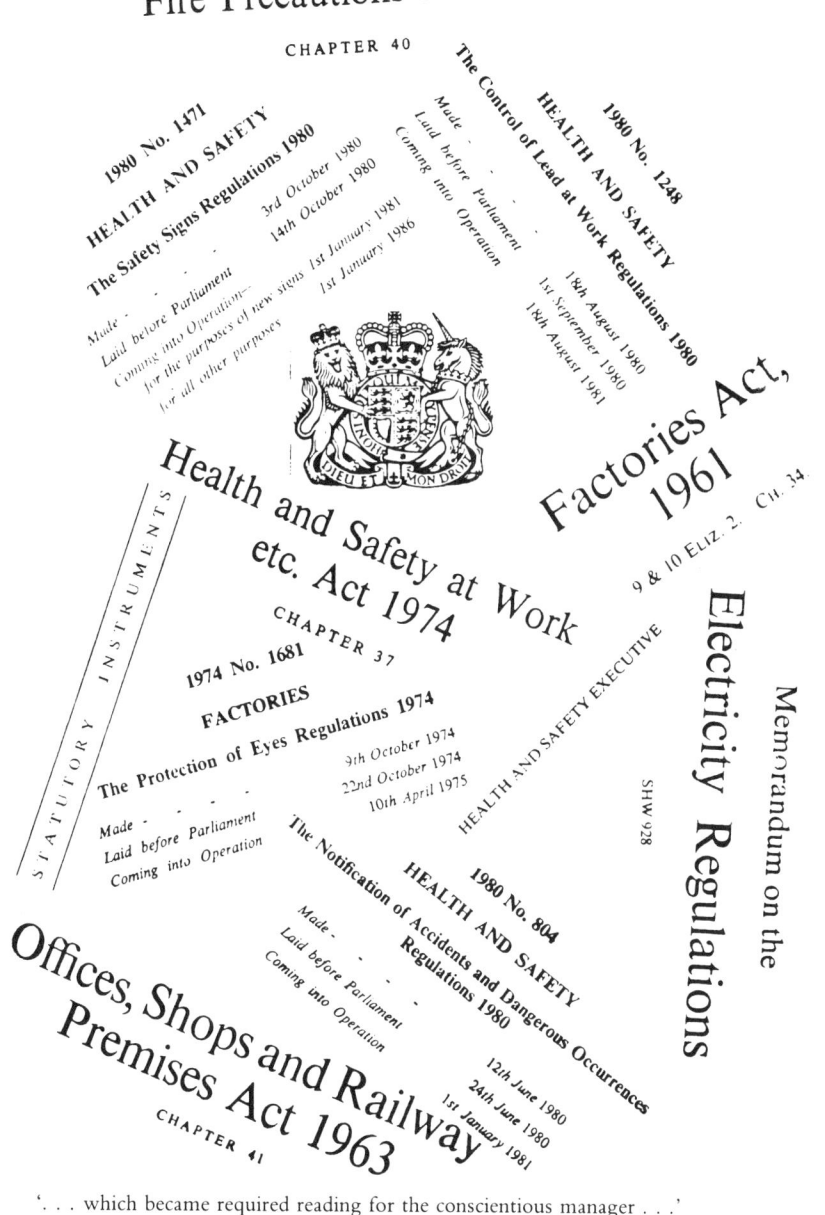

1980 No. 1471
HEALTH AND SAFETY
The Safety Signs Regulations 1980
Made - 3rd October 1980
Laid before Parliament 14th October 1980
Coming into Operation—
for the purposes of new signs 1st January 1981
for all other purposes 1st January 1986

The Control of Lead at Work Regulations 1980
1980 No. 1248
HEALTH AND SAFETY
Made - 18th August 1980
Laid before Parliament 1st September 1980
Coming into Operation 18th August 1981

Factories Act, 1961
9 & 10 Eliz. 2. Ch. 34

Health and Safety at Work etc. Act 1974
CHAPTER 37

STATUTORY INSTRUMENTS
1974 No. 1681
FACTORIES
The Protection of Eyes Regulations 1974
Made - 9th October 1974
Laid before Parliament 22nd October 1974
Coming into Operation 10th April 1975

HEALTH AND SAFETY EXECUTIVE

Electricity Regulations

Memorandum on the

SHW 928

The Notification of Accidents and Dangerous Occurrences Regulations 1980
1980 No. 804
HEALTH AND SAFETY
Made - 12th June 1980
Laid before Parliament 24th June 1980
Coming into Operation 1st January 1981

Offices, Shops and Railway Premises Act 1963
CHAPTER 41

'. . . which became required reading for the conscientious manager . . .'

– another factor to be added to the list when we consider the cost of accidents.

2.1.2 Statute Law

This is the law of the land, made by Parliament and enforced by government agencies. It includes the health and safety Acts and Regulations which periodically drop with a dull thud onto the desks of managers and which cause us to review our activities, procedures, policies and safety standards.

There are Acts of Parliament, which are the primary instruments of the law – for example, the Factories Act 1961, the Offices, Shops and Railway Premises Act 1963, the Fire Precautions Act 1971, the Health and Safety at Work etc. Act 1974.

There are, in addition, a wealth of Regulations which are made under the Acts. These generally apply to special situations, special hazards, particular operations, particular machines, special requirements, particular substances and even particular classes of employees. They are made as the need arises and they carry as much legal authority as the Acts under which they are made.

Some examples will illustrate the rich variety of the activities which they regulate – these are just a few:

Abrasive Wheels Regulations 1970.
Biscuit Factories Welfare Order 1927.
Carcinogenic Substances Regulations 1967.
Ionising Radiations (Sealed Sources) Regulations 1969.
Protection of Eyes Regulations 1974.
Safety Committees and Safety Representatives Regulations 1977.
Asbestos Regulations 1969.

A really authoritative reference book detailing relevant Acts, Regulations and the more important judgements made in the courts can be a worthwhile acquisition for the person who has responsibility for keeping his Company on the right side of the law. The one traditionally used by Health and Safety Executive Inspectors, professional Safety Officers, organisations which conduct safety courses and those people who need a definitive and compact reference is *Redgrave's Health and Safety in Factories*, published by Butterworths. It is not cheap, but excellence rarely is.

Another first class work of reference, in a somewhat different style, is *Croner's Health and Safety at Work*, from Croner Publications Ltd, Croner House, 173 Kingston Rd, New Malden, Surrey.

This is a loose-leaf binder of good quality, and the publishers provide a regular up-dating service.

2.2 The Factories Act 1961

This Act (and its associated Regulations) once formed the main thrust of industrial safety legislation applying to factories. The term 'factory' is defined in Section 175 of the Act, and premises which fall outside this definition are not regulated by the Act.

It is now seen as a decaying force, in that parts of it have been repealed and the remainder of its provisions will be similarly repealed, progressively, throughout future years. The same can be said of the Offices, Shops and Railway Premises Act 1963.

What remains, however, will continue in force alongside the more modern Health and Safety at Work Act 1974 (HSWA), and the associated Regulations will also continue in force until they, too, are selectively repealed or modified.

Much of the Factories Act 1961 deals clearly with specific hazards to safety and health in factories, and with minimum welfare standards. Thus, Parts 1, 2 and 3 list 'general provisions' with regard to such things as factory cleanliness, overcrowding, lighting, sanitary conveniences, machine guarding, dangerous substances, hoists and lifts, safe means of access, dangerous fumes, washing facilities, first-aid, examination of boilers, etc. so that legal requirements are spelled out and leave no room for argument.

There are a further ten Parts, dealing with welfare provisions, employment of omen and young persons, outworkers, pieceworkers, records and administration, offences and penalties, plus general items and Schedules.

It is not intended to provide a lengthy account of the 1961 Act in these pages – its provisions are being modified and in any event a piece of fundamental legislation which is 20 years old should not come as a bolt from the blue to any responsible manager. Those managers who don't have a copy, however, should repair the sad omission right away and should also buy a copy of the Factories Act 1961 (Repeals) Regulations 1976, from HMSO.

2.3 The Health and Safety at Work etc. Act 1974

This new approach to statutory regulation of the workplace was inspired by the Report of a Committee of Inquiry whose Chairman was Lord Robens.

The 'Robens Report', published in 1972, contained a comprehensive review of occupational safety and health legislation and conditions, and made recommendations for sweeping changes. It placed great emphasis on what was termed 'self-regulation' by employers, and also showed that health and safety problems were not confined only to the industrial scene – the general public, too, suffered from some of the activities of persons at work. As examples, the Report referred to atmospheric pollution, the dangers associated with transportation of hazardous substances, and other activities which impinge upon the safety of people outside the workplace.

The Report called for a greater degree of voluntary improvement by industry, plus more consultation and participation among employers and employees, and a larger emphasis to be placed upon codes of good practice rather than upon the outmoded and excessively detailed restrictions contained in many of the older Regulations.

The Report also pointed to the large number of people who were not protected by legislation existing at the time, since this legislation covered only those employees working in factories, offices, shops, mines, etc, as defined in the appropriate Acts.

In addition, it recommended that the various inspectorates which existed to administer safety provisions in different industries and disciplines (e.g. agriculture, alkali works, mines and quarries, factories, offices, etc.), should be unified under a new Authority whose membership would include representatives of employers, employees and other organisations.

The Robens Report was a fresh and searching wind of change which blew through the forest of existing legislation and rustled many dead branches. Its principles were quickly accepted by Parliament, and in 1974 the Health and Safety at Work Act (HSWA) received Royal Assent.

A comment appearing in Chapter 2 of the Robens Report is worth quoting: 'Promotion of safety and health at work is an essential function of good management. . . . Good intentions at board level are useless if managers further down the chain and closer to what happens on the shop floor remain preoccupied exclusively with production problems.'

This is a highly pertinent introduction to our examination of modern legislation.

The Health and Safety at Work Act was put on the statute book on 31st July 1974, and its stated purpose is:

(a) to secure the health, safety and welfare of persons at work,
(b) to protect persons other than persons at work against risks to health or safety arising out of or in connection with the activities of persons at work,
(c) to control the keeping and use of explosive, highly flammable or otherwise dangerous substances, and to generally prevent the unlawful acquisition, possession and use of such substances,
(d) to control the emission into the atmosphere of noxious or offensive substances from premises of any class prescribed for the purpose of this paragraph.

Unlike the Factories Acts, it doesn't go into any great detail regarding specific requirements for machine guarding, cranes, fire precautions, sanitary conveniences, gas holders, hoists and lifts, or other individual accident-producers. Instead, it provides broad guide-lines on the the duties of employers, employees, suppliers and users. It provides, also, for the making of future regulations and codes of practice, and sets out the framework of a policy-making body (the Commission) and a regulatory body (the Executive).

Following the Robens philosophy of 'self-regulation', the new Act stimulates and encourages higher standards of health and safety at the workplace by requiring employers and others to put their own house in order.

A very important departure from the earlier style of legislation is that HSWA applies to all 'persons at work' (including the self-employed), which means that about eight million people who were not previously covered are now embraced by the provisions of the Act. (An odd exception to this blanket of cover is the domestic servant in a private establishment – whilst the butler may be too discreet to demonstrate against this apparent slight, one wonders how the scullery maid feels, among her hazardous pots and pans!)

Some other significant features of HSWA are that it provides for the unification of the various Inspectorates (Mines, Electrical, Factories, Alkali, etc.) so that they now all come under the control of the Health and Safety Executive; it provides for the issue, by the Health and Safety Commission, of approved Codes of Practice; it demands the production and circulation, by the employer, of a Company Safety Policy, which encourages a great deal of self-assessment and self-regulation by managements.

All this in a 117-page paperback, published by Her Majesty's Stationery Office.

HSWA is divided into four Parts, headed as follows:

Part I. (53 pages) 'Health, Safety and Welfare in connection with Work, and Control of Dangerous Substances and Certain Emissions into the Atmosphere'.
Part II. (6 pages) 'The Employment Medical Advisory Service'. (EMAS)
Part III. (23 pages) 'Building Regulations and Amendment of the Building (Scotland) Act 1959'.
Part IV. (8 pages) 'Miscellaneous and General'.

There are, in addition, ten Schedules relating to matters contained within the body of the Act.

We certainly won't launch into a detailed review of HSWA in these pages; what we shall do, however, is look at some of the more important provisions – the ones which every manager should be well aware of and should be able to discuss with some confidence. We shall therefore work our way through some of the provisions of Part I of the Act, expanding upon some of the Sections in the order of their appearance in the text.

2.3.1 General Duties and Particular Duties (Section 2)

This Section spells out the duties of employers, and begins with a general duty which requires the employer 'to ensure, so far as is reasonably practicable, the health, safety and welfare at work of all his employees'. This is too broad a statement to be of sufficient guidance, so the remainder of the Section lists the *particular duties* which fall upon the employer's shoulders. These are as follows:

2(a) To provide and maintain plant and systems of work which are, so far as is reasonably practicable, safe and without risk to health.

2(b) To make arrangements to ensure, so far as is reasonably practicable, safety and absence of risk to health in connection with the use, handling storage and transport of articles and substances.

2(c) To provide such information, instruction, training and supervision as is necessary to ensure, so far as is reasonably practicable, the health and safety at work of his employees.

2(d) To maintain the place of work, and to provide and maintain access to and egress from it, which are, so far as is reasonably practicable, safe and without risk to health.

2(e) To provide and maintain a working environment for the employee which is, so far as is reasonably practicable, safe and without risk to health, and to provide adequate facilities for the employee's welfare at work.

These are basic and sensible requirements and if they were all complied with in the spirit, as well as in the letter, there would be very few accidents at the workplace. What this list of duties also achieves is the translation of our long-standing Common Law duties of care into binding statutory requirements.

The phrase 'so far as is reasonably practicable', you will have noticed, qualifies all the foregoing duties. This phrase is important, and needs some clarification.

In the various Acts and Regulations there are three levels of obligation placed upon the employer, depending upon the nature of the requirements. These must be carefully identified, when reading the texts, since they have a bearing upon the actions taken to comply with the law. These are expressed as follows:

(1) *Absolute* – something which must be done (or not done, as the case may be) without reservation or equivocation. For example, the 1961 Factories Act requirements for machinery guarding, which leave no room for excuses, are absolute.
(2) *'Where Practicable'* – something which must be done, if it is possible in the light of current knowledge and invention. This means that if it can be done, you must do it.
(3) *'Reasonably Practicable'* – in the case of Edwards versus N.C.B. (1949) the concept was illuminated in terms which said that 'a computation must be made, in which the quantum of risk is placed on one scale and the sacrifices involved in the measures necessary for averting the risk (whether in money, time or trouble) is placed on the other, and if it is shown that there is a gross disproportion between them – the risk being insignificant in relation to the sacrifice – then the defendants discharge the onus upon them'. (See *Redgrave's Health and Safety in Factories*, Butterworth & Co. (Publishers) Ltd.) In other words, the employer must balance the risk against the cost of eliminating the risk, and arrive at a sensible decision – which he must be ready to justify, in a court of law, when the crunch comes.

There might well, of course, be three quite different views taken of what is 'reasonably practicable'. The Factories Inspector will have one view, based on his hopefully wide experience of risks and remedies. The employer will certainly have another view, based upon *his* experience and upon the budget of his business. The unions will have *their* view, based upon the 'costs-don't-matter,-where-the-safety-of-our-members-is-involved' philosophy. You can't please all the people all the time.

We haven't finished with Section 2, yet, but this might be a convenient time to look back on the 'particular duties' and elaborate a little. Let's take them in the order in which they appear on the previous pages.

2.3.1.1 Safe plant, safe systems

Plant, and its ancillary equipment, are provided by the Company. We must accept that the hardware of our process is 'safe', since it has been designed, constructed and installed by people who are skilled at doing these things, and who have recourse to all the appropriate standards and codes. (Having said that, we must remember that unsafe design *can* exist – *people* cause accidents, and designers can use a pencil to create 'unsafe conditions'.)

However, as managers we can do little to modify the design of major items of plant and equipment – we have to work with what we're given. The operating manager, though, is quite entitled to point out any hazard created by bad design or construction – in fact he has a clear responsibility to protect the interests of his Company (and their employees) by doing so.

Having provided safe plant and equipment, the Company – through its managers, engineers and supervisors – must ensure that it remains safe. It must be *maintained* in a safe condition, to obviate risks to safety and health. Maintenance, adjustment, minor modification, etc. are normally the duties of supervisors, who request the work to be done and make the necessary arrangements.

With regard to safe systems of work, these are normally provided by management and it becomes the responsibility of the *supervisor* to maintain them. As a member of first-line management, the supervisor is closest to the man and his machine – he causes people to do things, he makes things happen, he regulates the conduct of employees; he therefore has the task of making sure that safe systems of work are operated. He must be given the guidance and the authority to carry out these duties.

The starting point in designing a safe system of work is to consider the potential hazards of the job, then to exercise control over them in order to neutralise or minimise them. There are several stages in this process.

(1) First, the hazard has to be clearly identified.
(2) Having identified the hazard, its potential must be assessed – i.e. the size of the problem must be measured.
(3) It is then necessary to select the method of controlling the hazard – i.e. by substitution, enclosure, use of personal protection, etc.
(4) The control system (the 'safe system of work') must then be designed, preferably documented and circulated, and fully implemented.
(5) The effectiveness of the system must then be monitored, to ensure that it *is* maintained, and that it is reviewed, modified or strengthened as the need arises.

Safe systems of work may include such items as permit-to-work, entry permit, electrical isolation, fork-truck driver training, machinery lock-off procedures; various codes, manuals, and rules for safe operation of equipment; emergency control plans; in fact, any formal and publicised systems which are designed to ensure efficient and safe conduct of the Company's operation. The operating manager is the natural custodian of safe systems of work.

2.3.1.2 *Use, handling, storage and transport*

This is a wide-ranging requirement of the Act and, again, management is the main agent of compliance. The magic words refer to 'articles and substances', and these cover almost anything one can think of. The requirements presuppose a thorough knowledge of all the activities, machines, chemicals, tools and equipment used in the workplace, together with a thorough appreciation of the hazards involved and the safeguards which are necessary to prevent accidents. No mean accomplishment for the man in charge of the shop!

He must ensure that articles and substances are used correctly and safely; that the correct principles of manual and mechanical handling are applied; that storage areas, loading bays, storage tanks and vessels, compounds, cabinets, stacks and stillages are monitored and kept safe; that the hazards of chemicals, raw materials, product, effluent, and all the other 'stuff' which abounds are recognised and controlled.

The computation of risks and remedies, enshrined within this part of the Act, is mind-boggling. But the manager must be prepared to cope, as part of his job.

2.3.1.3 *Information, instruction, training and supervision*

This is perhaps one of the most important activities of a conscientious management which is in direct control of plant and people.

It is people, at all levels, who cause accidents and plant malfunction. On the shop floor, people have to be influenced, guided, informed, instructed, monitored, supervised, corrected, trained, re-trained, and generally have their hands held throughout their working lifetime. The protection process begins when they clock-in on their first day with the Company, and it doesn't finish until they clock-out on their last day prior to retirement.

Employees have to be *told* about the hazards of the job, the process, the machines, the chemicals, the safety standards, the pitfalls and the precautions.

Employees have to be properly and clearly *instructed* in their duties, and given unequivocal direction in the performance of those duties, so that they know what is expected of them.

Employees have to be *trained* in the jobs they do, so that they know the correct and safe ways of doing what is expected of them.

Employees have to be *supervised* properly, to ensure that they carry out their duties in the manner demanded by the 'safe systems of work' which have been installed – and to ensure that they don't indulge in horseplay, short cuts, malpractice, variations from standard procedure, or any other unsafe conduct which can lead to accidents and losses.

In other words – and maybe a rude mnemonic might help to reinforce the message – what the Company must do is:

> **T**ell them.
> **I**nstruct them.
> **T**rain them.
> **S**upervise them.

2.3.1.4 *Safe place of work; safe means of access*

The employer's duty to provide a safe place of work is exercised through the design, construction, operation and supervision of the plant, premises, equipment and process over which he has control. The 'place of work' includes all the various places to which an employee has to go during the course of his duties, and a 'safe means of access' must be provided for him to get to and from these places. Having provided them, the employer must ensure that they remain safe.

'Access' covers a lot of ground, and can include access to valves, cocks, blankplates, vessels, staging, control gear, monitoring points, basement, roof, vehicle cabs, bunkers, locker rooms, clocking points, the mess room, the toilets – in fact, any place where his lawful duties may take him.

Such things as:

standing on handrails,
walking across single scaffold planks,
reaching across from ladders,
crossing rough, uneven ground,
stumbling over unlighted areas,
walking across railway sidings,
standing on office chairs,
jumping over pathway barriers,

– these are *not* safe means of access, and must not be condoned when seen to take place, since they are *unsafe acts*. The employer has a duty of care to his employees, to eliminate or correct such *unsafe conditions* as:

openings in floors, through which a person can fall,
pot-holes, cracked pavements, damaged roadways,
loose treads on stairways,
damaged ladders and steps,
obstructed walkways and gangways,
faulty or incomplete scaffolding,
untidy housekeeping standards, leading to trips and falls,
damaged or insecure handrails on stairways and platforms,
obstructed corridors leading to workrooms or escape exits,
and a whole range of items which come under the heading of 'means of access'.

Provide them safe, and *maintain* them safe – this is what the law demands of us.

2.3.1.5 Environment and welfare provisions

Provision of a safe and healthy working environment is obviously the prerogative of the employer, and it must be maintained through the delegated activities of supervisors.

The working environment will include such factors as:

Temperature – extremes of heat and cold.
Cleanliness of workrooms and work areas.
Atmosphere with regard to dust, fume, etc.
Noise both physical and psychological effects.
Space which must be adequate for persons working.

– In fact, the quality of the total working environment, in which an employee spends a third of his working lifetime. We must ensure that our employees are not frozen or given heatstroke; diseased by dirty conditions; choked by evil fumes or dangerous dust; deafened by harmful noise or driven insane by unwanted and preventable sounds; jammed into overcrowded workrooms or stifled by unbreathable and stuffy air in ill-ventilated work areas. So far as is reasonably practicable the working environment must be viable and safe and healthy.

With regard to employee welfare, we are not in the business of providing statutory parcels for pensioners, baskets of fruit on the top of the photocopier, or pop-music all over the workshop. Welfare, in this context, refers to basic statutory requirements such as sanitary accommodation, clean drinking water, washing facilities, sitting accommodation, locker space for clothing, adequate heating and drying space, and the standard requirements of an employee in a civilised place of work.

Section 2 of HSWA continues relentlessly, and lists further particular requirements, under sub-paragraph headings, dealing with Company Safety Policy, a machinery for the appointment of Safety Representatives, and for the setting up of joint safety committees within the workplace. These requirements are an interesting feature of modern safety legislation, since they again echo the Robens Report philosophy of 'self-regulation' and the sharing of accident prevention activities among employers and employees. Let us consider these requirements, and see what they involve.

2.3.1.6 Safety Policy

Section 2(3) (and an associated Regulation dealing with exemption, based upon the size of the workforce) requires that, where five or more persons are employed, the employer shall prepare a written statement of Company Safety Policy, which must be 'brought to the notice of' all his employees. This Policy must be revised, when necessary, and the revision must be publicised among the workforce.

It is not sufficient for the employer to produce a written policy which says, 'We will maintain a safe operation and cut down accidents' – the Policy must clearly spell out the employer's intentions with regard to health and safety, together with details of the organisation and the arrangements made for carrying out the Policy.

This is not just an example of legalistic bureaucrats gone on the rampage – the idea is that the employer will hopefully stop and think hard about the process, the hazards involved, the safe systems necessary to control the hazards, the quality and capability of his management team, the hardware at his disposal which may be necessary to safeguard his employees, and all the other factors involved in maintaining a safe enterprise. Only then should he put pen to paper and produce his Policy.

Having produced this commitment – and had it signed and dated by an appropriately senior person in the Company who has the authority to see it carried out – the employer should then distribute copies to all members of his workforce. Supervisors, in particular, will then be left in no doubt about *their* authority and responsibilities as outlined in management's statement of policy.

It might be useful to add that the Health and Safety Executive has produced guidance for its Inspectors on what to look for when inspecting and assessing a Company's Safety Policy. There has been a distinct shift in emphasis regarding the enforcement policy of the Executive. Whereas the Inspectors once concentrated on physical defects in plant and equipment which might lead to injury, they are now encouraged to assess management's ability to cope with safety problems, and the attitudes of people at all levels of society at the workplace. This assessment must inevitably include the attitude, capability, knowledge and performance of a Company's management staff.

2.3.1.7 *Safety Representatives and Committees (Section 2(4) (6) (7))*

Much anguish was generated among employers when the discussion document on union-appointed safety representatives was published by the Health and Safety Commission.

It was seen by some employers as a brutal infringement of their right to manage their own affairs, and an opening of the floodgates to union interference in matters for which management was ultimately responsible and accountable. Some union members, on the other hand, visualised the dawn of a new era in union power and capability, handed to them on a plate by Parliamentary decree.

The probability is that both factions are right and both are wrong. The legislation is pretty radical, and it will be some years before a proper assessment can be made of its influence on safety performance throughout the nation, and its impact on industrial relations in general.

Sufficient to say, at this stage, that the provisions exist as a fact of life and it is part of our duty to make them work successfully.

The statutory instrument which ushered in the new concept of rightful union involvement in safety and health was born of HSWA and is called the 'Safety Representatives and Safety Committees Regulations 1978' (SI 1977 No. 500). The Health and Safety Commission has published a useful booklet containing the regulations, a Code of Practice to complement them, plus Notes for Guidance, between its sombre brown covers. The Regulations themselves must be read with care, so that the full intention of the legislators is extracted from the written word. A copy of the 'brown booklet' is certainly an item of required reading by all concerned. What follows are simply notes on the broad outline of the Regulations:

(1) Recognised trade unions may appoint safety representatives from among the employees at the workplace. Appointment must be in writing to the employer, and must include the names of the appointees and the group or groups of employees whom they will represent. Appointment will cease if the union notifies the employer in writing, or if the representative resigns, or if he ceases to be employed at the workplace. Persons appointed must have been employed at the workplace, or at a similar employment, for at least two years.

(2) Appointed representatives will have the following functions:

- To represent the employees in consultation with the employer, on matters of health and safety.
- To investigate potential hazards and dangerous occurrences at the workplace, and to examine the causes of accidents.
- To investigate health and safety complaints by an employee whom he represents, and to make representations to the employer on such matters.
- To carry out inspections of the workplace in the following circumstances:

    (a) at intervals of three months (or more frequently, by agreement with the employer);

(b) where substantial change in conditions has occurred since the previous inspection, or when new information has been published, which might affect safety and health at the workplace;
(c) following a notifiable accident or dangerous occurrence at the workplace.

- To represent the employees, in workplace consultation with the Health and Safety Executive Inspector, and to receive relevant information from the Inspector.
- To attend safety committees, in his capacity as a safety representative.

It should be noted that whilst the safety rep. has a basketful of rights, he has no duties nor responsibilities placed upon him – unlike his employer, who carries a hefty burden at all times!

In addition to his functions, the safety rep. has the right to reasonable time off-the-job, without loss of pay, in order to attend safety committees, to perform his functions, and to receive training in the performance of those functions. He is also entitled to inspect certain documents relevant to the workplace or the group whom he represents, and to have copies of them, provided that these are documents which the employer is required to keep by health or safety statutes. (There are some documents which are excepted from this entitlement, and these are listed in the Regulations.)

Near the end of the Regulations is the requirement for the employer to set up a safety committee, if requested to do so in writing by two or more representatives. In doing so, the employer must consult with the reps. who made the request, and with representatives of the recognised trade union, regarding the way in which he proposes the committee should function. The committee must be established within three months of the request being made, and a notice must be posted at the workplace, stating the composition of the committee and the workplace which it will cover.

It will be easily appreciated, from the foregoing brief notes, that 'SI 500' is a potent and impact-laden piece of legislation, which can have potential for severe aggro or for great and lasting benefit – depending upon how the game is played by both sides. Many larger companies were well geared-up long before the Regulations were even thought of; safety committees existed; consultation and the open style of management were not a novelty. For these companies, a little adjustment to existing procedures was all that was needed. Other companies – perhaps the smaller ones, or those with more primitive ideas about safety consultation – were less happily placed, and the Regulations forced a sudden and possibly painful modification to their way of doing things.

In any event, the law remains inescapable and employers are chest-deep in its requirements.

Section 2 of HSWA then, with its general duties, its particular duties, and its off-shoot Regulations, is a highly important and comprehensive piece of accident-prevention machinery. But machinery needs service and maintenance, if it is not to break down. The Inspector of Factories will do what he can to keep a check on a Company's compliance with the law, but he cannot be in all places at once. It is up to management, therefore, to know the requirements and to comply with them – wholeheartedly supported by the supervisory team and by the employees.

There are other Sections of the Act which we must be aware of and must understand. What follows is just a small selection of the more important or interesting ones – the remainder are not unimportant, and management must do its homework on these, too.

2.3.2 Duties of Employees (Sections 7 and 8)

As was pointed out in a previous paragraph the employee, also, has *his* responsibilities. Being capable of independent thought and independent action, he must have some legal constraints placed upon him. The responsibilities of the employee are enshrined in Sections 7 and 8 of HSWA and it would be useful to quote these two Sections exactly as written in the Act:

Section 7: 'It shall be the duty of every employee while at work –

(a) to take reasonable care for the health and safety of himself and of other persons who may be affected by his acts or omissions at work; and

(b) as regards any duty or requirement imposed on his employer or any other person by or under any other statutory provisions, to co-operate with him so far as is necessary to enable that duty or requirement to be performed or complied with.'

Section 8: 'No person shall intentionally or recklessly interfere with or misuse anything provided in the interests of health, safety or welfare in pursuance of any of the relevant statutory provisions'.

These commonsense and fairly mild requirements go some small way toward balancing some of the employer's responsibilities with those of the employee.

'. . . unsafe acts which endanger himself or his colleagues . . .'

What it means is that the employee must not commit unsafe acts which might endanger himself or his colleagues or anyone else outside the workplace. And where the employer has duties imposed upon him by the law, then the employee must co-operate with the employer in complying with the requirements.

The other Section is shorter and more to the point – employees must not remove machine guards, fiddle with interlocks and other safety devices, make unauthorised modifications to safety equipment, throw his goggles down the toilet or take a pick-axe to the locker room and smash all the wash basins. The wording of the Section, however, suggests that in many workplaces, he can turn his safety helmet into a flower-pot, if he wants to, since it's not provided 'in pursuance of any of the relevant statutory provisions'.

The duty of the employee to act safely and to use, rather than abuse, those things which are provided for safety and health is not confined to the Act. Similar requirements are found in many of the Regulations, where it is often stated that the employee must co-operate with the employer in carrying out the duties specified.

This is illustrated, for example, in the Protection of Eyes Regulations – of which more later.

It must be emphasised, however, that the duties placed upon employees do *not* relieve the employer of *his* duties of care to those people employed by him. There are no loopholes.

'. . . to use, rather than abuse, those things which are provided for his safety . . .'

2.3.3 The Commission and the Executive (Section 10)

This Section of the Act makes provision for the setting up of two bodies corporate, called the 'Health and Safety Commission', and the 'Health and Safety Executive'.

The Commission consists of a Chairman, appointed by the Secretary of State, with not less than six nor more than nine other members. Before appointing these other members, the Secretary of State must consult with organisations which represent employers, employees, and local authority/professional bodies. This sort of consultation will hopefully result in a Commission membership which has regard for the interests of a broad band of the working population and their employers.

The Commission becomes responsible for assisting and encouraging research into health and safety matters, and for publicising the results; for fostering training and providing advice and information; for making proposals for new health and safety Regulations, and for publishing discussion documents on such proposals; for initiating or approving relevant codes of practice; for appointing advisory committees on health and safety matters; and for directing the activities of the Executive.

The Executive consists of a Director, appointed by the Commission, and two other members who are appointed by the Commission after consultation with the Director. This three-man body is responsible for appointing its Inspectors, for administering the Inspectorate, and for enforcing the Act and its Regulations.

As was noted earlier, the various Inspectors who previously dealt with health and safety aspects in diverse areas of industry – factories, mines and quarries, alkali, radiological, construction, electrical, etc. – have now been brought together under the unifying executive body, and are called Health and Safety Executive Inspectors.

2.3.4. Powers of Inspectors (Sections 20–25)

The image which people tend to carry of the dreaded 'Factory Inspector' seems to vary from person to person, and it's usually false.

Some see him as a creeping, spying, devious little Civil Servant who spends his time peeking into odd corners of the workplace, looking for ways to be officious and obstructive.

Others see him as some sort of governmental Genghis Khan, ten feet tall and drunk with unbridled power, intent upon throwing people into jail and closing down their business.

Neither of these impressions is true; the average Inspector is well trained, highly experienced, well versed in accident prevention techniques and the law, a model of polite rectitude, discreet, and generously helpful. He would prefer to assist than to prosecute, and is fanatically incorruptible.

Having said that, let's now examine his powers under the Act, and see what authority he has over our activities at work:

'. . . a creeping, spying, devious little civil servant . . .'

(a) He may enter any premises which come into his field of responsibility at any reasonable time of day – or at any time, if he has reason to believe that something dangerous is going on within.
(b) If he has reasonable cause to believe that he may be obstructed in the execution of his duty, he may take a police constable with him.

The Health and Safety at Work etc. Act 1974

'... some sort of governmental Genghis Khan, ten feet tall and drunk with unbridled power...'

(c) He may also take with him any other person duly authorised by his own enforcing authority, and any equipment or materials necessary for the purposes of inspection, investigation, or of other purposes.
(d) He may direct that any premises, or any part of them, or anything within them, shall be left undisturbed for the purposes of investigation or examination.
(e) He may take such measurements, photographs or recordings as may be necessary for the purposes of investigation or examination.
(f) He may take samples of any articles or substances found in the premises, or samples of the atmosphere in or around the premises.
(g) He may cause any article or substance to be dismantled or subjected to test, if he considers it to be the cause or the potential cause of danger to safety or health.
(h) He may take possession of such article or substance, and keep it for as long as is necessary to carry out examination of it, or to ensure that it is not tampered with before it has been examined by him, or to ensure that it is available as evidence in any proceedings for an offence under any statutory provision.
(i) He may require any person to answer such questions as he thinks are necessary, and to require that person to sign a declaration of the truthfulness of the answers given. (But the person's answers may not be used as evidence against him in any subsequent proceedings.)
(j) He may inspect and take copies of any books or documents which are necessary for him to see for the purposes of investigation or inspection.
(k) He may require any appropriate person to afford him such facilities and assistance as may be necessary to enable him to exercise the powers conferred upon him.

It is obvious, then, that the Inspector has a wide range of powers which He can exercise in the performance of His duties. Managements would be well advised to treat Him with respect, to assist Him in His duties, and to obstruct Him not in the performance thereof, lest in His wrath He cause all Hell to break loose!

Remember, though, that the Inspector who abuses these powers, or attempts to use them unnecessarily, is a very rare example of the species. In the main, Inspectors are courteous and helpful, and the Inspectorate is a mine of information on health and safety matters. Advice on accident prevention is readily available, and quickly forthcoming upon request.

2.3.4.1 Improvement and Prohibition Notices

Under the new Act, there are two additional and very significant powers which the Inspector has collected – and has used to good effect. They enable him to take prompt preventive action, without having to suffer the delays of making applications to the courts or of having to await prosecution proceedings. These powers enable him to issue Improvement or Prohibition Notices upon persons or Companies, and they work as follows:

Improvement Notice. If the Inspector is of the opinion that a person is contravening or has contravened a relevant statutory provision, he may serve upon that person a Notice which requires that the contravention shall be remedied within a specified period of time.

Prohibition Notice. If the Inspector discovers an activity which is being, or is about to be, carried on, and which he thinks will involve risk of imminent and serious injury, he may serve a Notice prohibiting that activity forthwith.

These Notices can be served upon any person with whom responsibility rests, or who is undertaking the activity, whether he is an employer or an employee. There are other details surrounding the issue of these Notices, and the details are enshrined in Sections 21 to 24 inclusive. Companies should be well acquainted with the additional technicalities involved. They deal with appeals against the Notices; the specification of remedies contained within them; the time limits or the immediacy which can be imposed; the particulars which Notices must contain.

2.3.5 Approved Codes of Practice (Sections 16 and 17)

The purpose of a Code of Practice is to give guidance on the health and safety aspects of an activity, the standards of manufacture or use of certain equipment, the code of conduct relating to certain situations, or criteria of a similar nature. There can be Industry Codes, such as those produced by leading petrochemical Companies, dealing with their products or installations. There can be British Standard Codes, dealing with a variety of esoteric matters. There can be purely domestic codes, tailored to suit the needs of a particular Company, and dealing with particular aspects of safety within that Company. Or there can be what is now called an *Approved Code of Practice.*

Section 16 of the Act provides for the Health and Safety Commission to approve and issue Codes of Practice, the stated purpose of which is 'to provide practical guidance on health and safety regulations or any of the existing statutory provisions . . .'.

Before seeking consent from the Secretary of State to approve and issue such Codes, the Commission must consult with any government departments or other bodies as may be appropriate.

The Commission may approve Codes from sources other than themselves, if they consider these to be suitable for the stated purpose.

Once it has been 'approved' by the Commission, a Code of Practice assumes a rather peculiar legal status. Failure to observe the provisions of a Code is not in itself an offence – but where a person is accused of breaking a statutory provision, the fact that he failed to observe the relevant Code of Practice may be taken as evidence that he failed to do all that was reasonably practicable to comply with the statutory requirements.

This quasi-legal status of an Approved Code of Practice is spelt out in Section 17 of the Act – though it takes three sub-sections, two sub-sub-sections, or 29 lines of mind-blowing legal parlance to get the message across.

An interesting feature of the Commission's 'brown book' dealing with Safety Representatives is that it contains, in one single publication, an example of:

(a) *Regulations* – which are statutory requirements and form part of the law of the land,
(b) *Approved Codes of Practice* – which are what we've just been looking at, and
(c) *Guidance Notes* – which, though issued by a body as august as the Commission, have no legal standing at all.

It is likely that Approved Codes of Practice will, in the future, feature strongly in the tenets of health and safety at the workplace. It is to be hoped that they will be written in a clearer form of language than the strangled prose which distinguishes much of the Act and its Regulations.

It must be emphasised, once more, that what has been written about the Health and Safety at Work Act in these pages has merely scratched the surface of the beast. The full text of the Act contains 85 Sections, and there are 10 Schedules in addition. The whole thing forms part of any manager's list of required reading.

Part 3
Sundry Subjects

The items covered in this part of the book comprise a miscellaneous collection of which employers and employees should have a working knowledge. They are not intended to cover the whole spectrum of safety know-how, but are simply representative of the problems and procedures which colour the working day of people who have to earn their living in industry.

They are drawn from commonsense and from Regulations – two sources which are not by any means incompatible, if the latter are read and understood in the light of the former!

3.1 Training-out Accidents

The Health and Safety Executive, along with officers of an employer's insurers, learned judges on the bench, safety societies and councils, related faculties of universities and other safety institutions all recognise and emphasise the value of effective and appropriate job-training.

Training is one of the most – perhaps *the* most – important and valuable components of any accident prevention programme. Taken to its logical conclusion, it can eliminate unsafe acts and unsafe conditions, so that accidents can be 'trained-out' of existence.

If you believe this to be an impossible ambition, then the proposition that *people* cause accidents hasn't been understood and accepted. Let us therefore consider the fact that if *everybody* was properly trained in the correct and safe way of doing his job, there would be no unplanned events, no mistakes, no short-cuts, no neglect of responsibility, no lack of knowledge, no unsafe methods of work, no technical blunders, no faults in manufacture, no errors in the use of equipment – no accidents, in fact. 'Everybody', of course, includes the designer, the manufacturer, the engineer, the chemist, the architect, the builder, the manager, the supervisor, the employee, and a whole mob of other people who create activity and conditions at the workplace and outside it.

The nearer one gets to the actual performance of workplace activities, the closer one gets to accident potential or accident involvement. (If you do absolutely nothing, then not much can happen to you!) The employee therefore (placed, as he is, at the sharp end of the business) is the person most in need of thorough training. He must be properly trained in every aspect of his job, so that he can perform profitably, efficiently, effectively, and safely – not necessarily in that order of priority, but then profit, efficiency, effectiveness and safety are all accepted as being spokes in the wheel of success, and when the wheel spins the spokes are barely distinguishable from each other.

Training is not a 'job-and-finish' exercise. It's a continuous, continuing process; ask any professional, and he'll agree this is so. It involves such elements as induction training, job training, refresher training, change-of-job training, new methodology training, new-technology or equipment training – and even, in these enlightened times, training for retirement. We live in a changing world, where techniques and methods of work are in a state of constant development. Training must keep pace with this change, if we are to do our jobs properly.

The systematic training and development of a Company's workforce is one of the manager/supervisor's responsibilities, and it has to be properly planned, executed, monitored, and up-dated when necessary. When carried out, the date, duration, content, level and results of the training must be recorded for future reference. This is particularly true of safety training, the records of which could be asked for by a Health and Safety Executive Inspector, or a judge, or the Insurance Company's solicitor, in the event of serious injury to an employee.

The elements of an effective training programme are not difficult to identify. They are:

(a) *Job Analysis* – defining what a person has to do and know, in order to perform his task efficiently and safely. The job can be looked at in its entirety if the activities are simple and straightforward with little variation from a set pattern. If the job is more complex, then it can be broken up into sub-divisions or segments, and these can be analysed separately. The important thing is that the whole job is examined, in all its aspects, so that the training needs of each segment are established.

(b) *Programme Preparation* – a careful consideration of training

objectives; of how these objectives can best be achieved; of the best sequence of presentation to achieve a smooth and logical flow of information and training; of the best type of presentation to achieve clarity of training information and acceptance of the information presented; of the time-scale involved, to ensure that sufficient time is spent with the trainee to enable him to learn the job before being turned loose at the workplace.
(c) *Implementation of the Programme* – so that the training is carried through efficiently, positively, enthusiastically, under proper supervision, and always with regard to the objectives which have been formulated during the programme preparation stage.
(d) *Monitoring and Review* – so that the results of the programme can be evaluated, to see if objectives have been achieved; so that any shortfall can be identified, and the programme modified to correct this; so that we know we're getting 'value for money' from the programme as a whole.

Training, then, must not be entered into lightly – it is an essential part of any good Company's management policy and objectives.

One of the most important aspects of training, from the health and safety point of view, is *Safety Induction*. When an employee joins a Company, he is usually inexperienced in the particular hazards of the job he is going to do. He must therefore be taken aside, on his very first day, and given good hard information about the hazards, the safeguards, the safe working methods, the safety equipment he must use, the things he mustn't do, the facilities provided for him, the conduct expected of him, the policy of the Company, and all the other safety-related subjects.

Safety induction training must be planned and executed in the same careful way as any other sort of training, and will properly include 'chalk-and-talk', practical instruction, written hand-out material, periodical review, and of course the maintenance of proper records to show what has been done and when it was done.

Every employer must periodically search his soul in order to satisfy himself that the people under his control are receiving adequate training – and if not satisfied, he must do something about it. He owes it to his employees, and to his own conscience, to do this.

3.2 Machine Guarding

There are very few workplaces where machines have no part to play in the business. Not only in factories, but in offices, shops, service stations, theatres, hotels, restaurants, railway stations, airports, docks, warehouses, stores, parks and gardens, farms, forests and dairies – machinery of some type plays a role in the activities of the day. It is a familiar and useful entity, essential, commonplace, labour-saving – and lethal!

The Health and Safety Executive's famous museum at Horseferry Road (now, sadly, no longer in existence) held a macabre selection of machines, many of them still decorated with blood-stains, pieces of tattered clothing and hanks of human hair; mute testimony to the rending, tearing, crushing power of a piece of unguarded machinery in which some unfortunate employee had become entangled.

Compared with a machine the flesh is weak, as many people have discovered to their cost, and the sheer awfulness of a machine accident has invested machine guarding with a traditionally high degree of importance.

The 1961 Factories Act devotes nine Sections to the danger of machines, the best known of which are Sections 12, 13 and 14, which demand secure fencing of dangerous parts. ('Fencing', incidentally, is a throwback from earlier days, when chestnut stave fences were erected around certain machines, to keep people away – we call them machine guards, now!)

These Sections of the 1961 Act are quite absolute in their requirements; there is no question of reasonable practicability, or convenience, or any qualifying ifs or buts. The words are *'shall be securely fenced'*, and the one let-out says 'unless it is in such a position or of such construction as to be as safe to every person employed or working on the premises as it would be if securely fenced'. This is the concept of safety by position, and is most certainly not to be relied upon. Very few machines are 'safe by position' – even a piece of gearing perched on a ledge twenty feet up the wall has to be approached at some time, by somebody, for lubrication or maintenance or inspection. so it's better to forget the 'safe by position' myth, and have it securely fenced.

Sections 12, 13 and 14 of the old Act refer to machinery in the logical sequence of prime movers, transmission machinery, and other machinery.

The term *prime mover* refers to every engine, motor, electric generator, rotary converter, flywheel, or other appliance which provides mechanical energy derived from steam, electricity, water, wind, the combustion of fuel, or any other source. In other words, the bit that makes the machine go.

Transmission machinery refers to every drum, clutch, belt, pulley, shaft, coupling, or other device which transmits the prime mover's power to the machine being driven.

Other machinery refers to all driven machines which are not included in the first two categories, and Section 14 demands the secure fencing of all their dangerous parts. If the machine cannot be securely fenced, then it may be protected by an approved automatic device which prevents the exposure of a dangerous part whilst in motion, or which 'stops the machine forthwith in case of danger'. That is, where fixed guarding is impossible, then such things as automatic guards (as used on power presses) or safety interlocks (which stop the machine automatically if a gate is opened or if a person passes through a fixed photoelectric light beam, etc.) may be used.

In any event, there must be no possibility of a person coming into contact with a dangerous moving part of a machine.

The meaning of 'dangerous part' has been handed down to us with commendable clarity from the judges' bench in the course of two important judgements:

(1) A dangerous part of a machine is one which might be 'a reasonably foreseeable cause of injury to anybody acting in a way in which a human being may be reasonably expected to act, in circumstances which may be reasonably expected to occur' (John Summers versus Frost, 1955).
(2) And if, 'in the ordinary course of human affairs, danger may reasonably be anticipated from its use unfenced, not only to the prudent, alert and skilled operative intent upon his task but also the careless and inattentive operative whose inadvertent or indolent conduct may expose him to risk of injury or death from the unguarded part'. (Mitchell versus North British Rubber Co. Ltd, 1945).

These are highly important judgements, and they clearly indicate that we cannot place the onus on any person not to poke his finger into a machine to see if it's dangerous. When that person finds out the hard way, then the main responsibility is management's because the fool shouldn't have been able to do it anyway.

Machine guarding is one of the basics of safety, and must be a prime responsibility of the Company. People are funny creatures – they would often prefer to remove guards or deliberately defeat interlocks and other safety systems, just to make their job a little bit easier. When they get their fingers chopped off, they then assume an expression of outrage and hammer on the doors of the court, demanding compensation! Management has the onerous duty of protecting fools from themselves, and protecting the Company from the activities of fools.

The British Standards Institution Code of Practice No. 5304, *Safeguarding of Machinery*, spells out in great detail the standards required in the design and quality of machine guards. It is this Standard to which the Executive Inspector will refer when assessing the suitability of a guard or an automatic safety device. As a vital volume of reference, it appears on our list of essential reading.

As a summarising generality, the message is that a person should not be able to get himself caught in any dangerous part of a machine, whether he wants to or not. The employer must see that he can't.

Another (less expensive) reference for the busy manager or engineer is a short booklet entitled *Machine Guarding*, published by the British Safety Council. It contains a wealth of excellent drawings and explanatory texts, illustrating the traps and hazards of machinery, together with the types of guards which overcome the problems. As a working reference, this publication is a very sound investment.

3.3 Machinery Attendants

There exists a broad misconception that a Machinery Attendant is someone who works with machinery, or someone who can do things to machines without bothering about guards because he's experienced, or qualified, or something. Thus, there are some fitters and machinists who believe they have magic powers which protect them from drill spindles and from the law. This is not the case, and people who think it is are sadly mistaken. The Machinery Attendant is a special person, appointed by the Company to perform a special duty, in special and specified circumstances.

Having dealt at length with secure fencing of machinery in Sections 12, 13 and 14, the Factories Act then goes on to acknowledge (in Section 15) that certain things have to be done which apparently contravene the requirements of the previous three Sections.

Section 15 is entitled *Provisions as to Unfenced Machinery*, and it refers to lubrication, examination and subsequent necessary adjustment of the part whilst the machinery is in motion, under conditions specified in 'regulations made by the Minister'.

The regulations referred to are the *Operations at Unfenced Machinery Regulations, 1946*, and those concerned should know them and understand them thoroughly. What follows is a brief outline of the Regulations.

A Machinery Attendant must be aged 18 years or over, and must have had sufficient training, in the work which he has to do, to be properly aware of the dangers arising from it. He must be appointed by Management, given a Certificate of Appointment, and his name must be entered in, or attached to, the statutory General Register.

He must be familiar with the Regulations, and must be given a copy of the prescribed leaflet (Factory Form F.280) which deals with the dangers and the precautions associated with moving machinery.

The circumstances under which a certificated Machinery Attendant may approach unfenced moving machinery are as follows:

(a) Where it becomes necessary to examine part of the machinery, and this cannot be done with the machinery at rest or with the guard in position.
(b) Where such examination shows that lubrication or adjustment is immediately necessary and this cannot be done with the machinery at rest or with the guard in position.
(c) Where it becomes necessary to lubricate – or to mount or ship belts on moving pulleys associated with – such transmission machinery as is specified in a Schedule to the Regulations, but *only* if such activities *cannot* be postponed until the machinery can be stopped without detriment to the process.

Therefore, if a Machinery Attendant is able to carry out his duties with the machine at rest, then he must do so – his certificate of appointment does *not* allow him to approach an unfenced machine in motion simply for the sake of convenience.

When a Machinery Attendant is carrying out his duties, the following rules apply:

He must wear a single-piece, close-fitting suit of overalls, without external pockets other than a hip pocket, and fastened by a method which allows no loose ends.

A second person must be available, within sight or hearing, who knows what action to take in the event of emergency.

Steps must be taken – including the erection of a barrier, if this is appropriate and reasonably practicable – to prevent any other person from being exposed to danger from the machinery.

Any ladder which he is using must be securely lashed, or must be firmly held by a second person.

Where belts are being handled on a moving pulley, the following rules apply:
Secure hand-holds and foot-holds must be afforded. There must be reasonable clearance between the pulley and any fixed structure.

The belt must be less than 6 inches in width – and if over 4 inches in width, it must already have been used on its pulley. It must have a joint which is either laced, or is flush with the belt surface, and must be in a good state of repair in all respects.

All belts used in the processes specified in the Schedule to the Regulations, and which are likely to be handled at a moving pulley, must be inspected daily (from a safe position) by a competent person, and any repair found necessary must be carried out as soon as practicable.

It will be seen from the foregoing that before a Machinery Attendant is permitted to approach unfenced moving machinery, the following three questions should be considered:

(1) Must the examination be carried out with the machinery in motion, or can it be stopped for this purpose?
(2) Is adjustment or lubrication immediately necessary, and if so does it *have* to be done with the machinery in motion?
(3) Is the transmission machinery in question included in the Schedule of Continuous Processes, and if so can lubrication or the handling of belts be postponed until the machinery can be stopped 'without detriment to the process'?

Proper consideration of these questions will reveal that if the Machinery Attendant can perform his duties with the machinery at rest and/or properly guarded, then he must do so.

3.4 Highly Flammable Liquids (HFL) and LPG

Nature has provided us – through the medium of the petrochemicals and solvents industries – with a burgeoning range of liquid fuels, solvents, liquefied gases and other imperatives of a modern lifestyle. Our civilisation (for want of a better word) would grind to a shuffle without them, so we have to use them in order to maintain our status as a highly developed society. The price we pay for having them on tap is enormous – not least in the area of safety, since they tend to catch fire easily, burn enthusiastically, and create spectacular havoc and devastation in a very short time. The famous Flixborough episode is a case in point!

The problem with highly flammable liquids, and with liquefied petroleum gases, is that they vaporise very quickly, when they get out of the cage, and slink off as an invisible cloud in search of a source of ignition. Then the balloon really goes up. There is an excellent training film on the market, called *'Highly Flammable Liquids – Beware'*, which graphically illustrates this point. It demonstrates what can happen in a workplace – whether it's a major industrial complex or a back-street bucket-shop – when procedures become sufficiently neglected to permit casual risks to be taken by careless people.

There are very few establishments where flammable liquids of some sort are not stored or used, so the risk is spread pretty widely. The regulations governing our handling of them, therefore, apply to most of us. In June 1973 the Regulations became effective. They are called, naturally enough, the *Highly Flammable Liquids and Liquefied Petroleum Gases Regulations, 1972* and they make statutory provisions for storage, marking, use, prevention of spillage, fire precautions, disposal, and ventilation of premises.

A highly flammable liquid is defined as any liquid which gives off a flammable vapour at temperatures less than 32°C. Liquefied Petroleum Gas is defined as a commercial butane, a commercial propane, or any mixture of these. What follows is a much condensed version of the Regulations. For a proper appreciation of its many requirements, the operating manager should obtain a copy from HMSO and study it carefully.

Reg. 5 – storage – All HFL must be stored:

(a) In suitable fixed storage tanks, in safe positions.
(b) In suitable closed vessels, kept in a store-room which is either a fire-resisting structure or which is in a safe position.
(c) In suitable closed vessels, kept in a safe position in the open air, protected where necessary against strong sunlight.
(d) In the case of a workroom, where the total quantity does not exceed 50 litres, in suitable closed vessels kept in a bin or cabinet of fire-resisting structure.

Regulation 5 does not apply to HFL in the fuel tank of a vehicle, nor to any suitable small vessel containing less than 500 ml. In (a), (b) and (c) above, steps must be taken to ensure that any spillage is safely contained, or immediately drained off to a suitable container, or otherwise treated to make it safe.

Reg. 6 – marking – Every store-room, bin, cupboard, tank or vessel which is used for storing HFl must be clearly and boldly labelled 'Highly Flammable', or 'Flashpoint Below 32°C', or with an otherwise appropriate indication of flammability. Where this is impracticable, then the legend 'Highly Flammable Liquid' must be conspicuously displayed as close to the place as possible.

Regulation 6 does not apply to fuel tanks of vehicles, nor to places which contain spirits intended for human consumption.

Reg. 7 – LPG Storage and Marking – LPG which is not in use shall be stored:

(a) In suitable underground reservoirs, or in suitable fixed tanks or vessels which are situated in a safe position in the open air.
(b) In suitable movable storage tanks or vessels, kept in a safe position in the open air.
(c) In the pipelines, pumps, or other appliances which form part of a totally enclosed system.
(d) In suitable cylinders, kept in a safe place in the open air or (where this is not practicable) kept in a store-room constructed of non-combustible material. The store-room must be either in a safe position, or must be a fire-resisting structure used only for the storage of LPG or acetylene cylinders.

No LPG shall be present in any workplace, other than in suitable cylinders or pipelines, and the number of such cylinders or pipelines shall be as small as is reasonably practicable.

LPG cylinders must be *properly stored* (see (d) above) when not in use, and empty cylinders must be removed from the workplace to be stored or refilled without delay.

Every tank, vessel, cylinder and store-room used for storing LPG must be clearly and boldly marked 'Highly Flammable – LPG'. Where this is impracticable, then the legend must be conspicuously displayed as close to the place as possible. (This does not apply to LPG in vehicle fuel tanks, nor to any suitable small vessel containing less than 500 ml of LPG.)

Reg. 8 – Spills and Leaks – Where HFL is to be conveyed within a factory, it shall be done by means of a totally enclosed system of pipes and pumps. Where this is not reasonably practicable, then vessels must be used which are designed and constructed so as to avoid the risk of spillage or leakage.

The quantity of HFL present in any workplace at any one time must be as small as is reasonably practicable, having regard to the process being carried on.

All practicable steps must be taken to prevent spillage or leakage, and all tanks and vessels must be kept closed except as necessary for manufacture, manipulation or use of their contents.

Where movable HFL tanks or vessels have been emptied, they must be removed to a safe place or properly stored (as indicated in the appropriate Regulations above) unless they are to be immediately refilled or have been made free from HFL vapour.

Reg. 9 – Sources of Ignition – Where a dangerous concentration of HFL vapour is likely to be present, there must be no means likely to cause ignition.

In such areas, any cotton waste or other material which is contaminated with HFL, or is liable to spontaneous combustion, must be placed in a suitable metal container which has a suitable metal cover, or must be removed to a safe place without delay.

Reg. 10 – Escape of Vapour – This Regulation requires steps to be taken to prevent the escape of vapour into the atmosphere. It requires work to be carried on within cabinets or enclosures which are fire-resistant and have exhaust ventilation, so that vapour does not build up in the workroom. Where this is not practicable, then the workroom itself must have adequate exhaust ventilation.

Reg. 14 – Smoking – There shall, of course, be no smoking in places where HFL is present, and the Company must ensure that this rule is properly publicised and complied with.

Reg. 15 – Ignition and Burning – With certain exceptions, no HFL shall be ignited other than in plant or apparatus which is suitable for the purpose, and by the proper use of the plant or apparatus. The exceptions to this requirement are:

(a) Where the sole purpose is the disposal of waste, in which case it must be burned in suitable plant or apparatus.
(b) By a competent person, in a safe manner.
(c) To provide persons with fire-fighting training, when it must be done in a safe manner and under the continuous superversion of a competent person.

Reg. 17 – Fire Fighting – Where HFL is manufactured or used, there must be provided and maintained sufficient and appropriate means of fighting a fire, and this must be readily available and properly placed.

Reg. 18 – Duties of Employed Persons – All employees must comply with the requirements of those Regulations which relate to them, and must report without delay any defect in plant, equipment or appliance.

It will be seen, from the foregoing paragraphs, that the Company has a formidable list of duties to comply with in relation to highly flammable liquids and liquefied petroleum gases. These duties inevitably involve the manager or supervisor who has direct charge of the workplace in which these substances are used or stored. It pays dividends, therefore, to look around the area in which you work with a fresh eye, to see if any of the Regulations have been missed.

In doing this, *don't just consider the highly flammable liquids by definition* – there are plenty of flammable or easily ignitable chemicals and other things which need looking at, in addition to those with a flash point of 32°C or less. Oils, light greases, paint, aerosols, cylinders of flammable gas, plastics, polish and wax – our workplaces are liberally dotted with cupboards and storage areas which contain all sorts of things that go whoomph in the night. It's too late to take precautions when the fire alarm is sounding!

3.5 Asbestos – the stealthy killer

Some years ago the media enjoyed an orgy of hysteria about asbestos, and in the process our newspapers and television injected a fair amount of dread into the minds of workpeople and provided the unions with a fine opportunity to bellow their disgust, look shocked, and create new restrictive practices.

The trouble stemmed, it seems, from conditions in certain places where asbestos was manipulated, processed and used on a large scale – creating large concentrations of fibres and dust which employees inhaled over a very long period. As a result, some were made very ill and some died of lung diseases.

These illnesses take a long time to reveal themselves, and this is a characteristic of many carcinogenic substances – the effects are felt only after many years of exposure. We were late in discovering the harmful effects of asbestos dust, and in fairness to employers it is only during the past decade or two that sufficient information came to light. We now know the facts, and we now have Regulations to control the hazards of asbestos in the working environment.

It is a tragic aspect of industrial progress that we often discover harmful features of a product or a process only when it's too late to save the lives of those who have been exposed to those features.

The story of asbestos is one such tragedy.

There are three main types of asbestos:

Chrysotile – 'white asbestos', which is the most widely used, and which comprises about 95% of all asbestos produced.
Amosite – a grey or brown variety, of which very little is used.
Crocidolite – 'blue asbestos', which is no longer imported into the UK as a raw material, but which may still exist as a constituent of insulation in older installations or where it has been used in combination with other materials for its acid-resistant properties.

Asbestos has a variety of applications and can be seen in many forms. As cloth and textiles, used for fire blankets, fire curtains, fire-resistant gloves, jointing material. As rope and cord, for jointing, packing, etc. As asbestos cement products, roof sheeting, guttering, rain-water down pipes, floor tiles, insulation boards, etc. in the building industry. As asbestos-reinforced plastics and bonded asbestos items, clutch and brake linings, electrical insulators, battery cases. As thermal insulation, when mixed with fillers and applied to hot surfaces such as boilers, steam pipes. In fact, we cannot do without asbestos altogether – it plays too important a part in our lives. Substitution is a possibility, on a limited scale.

The vital safeguard in dealing with asbestos is to prevent the generation of dust or, where this is not entirely possible, to preclude the basic philosophy of the 1969 Asbestos Regulations (SI No. 690), which contains a host of requirements for handling asbestos safely and for maintaining exposure levels at the workplace which are not in excess of certain specified concentrations.

Since that date, however, control limits have been progressively reduced and the Health and Safety Executive has issued additional and revised guidance notes, plus Regulations which require the licensing and control of contractors who carry out the stripping and removal of existing asbestos materials on site, and which ban the marketing and use of certain types of asbestos.

Control limits for asbestos dust in the workplace atmosphere are currently set at the following levels:

(a) For dust consisting of, or containing, Crocidolite or Amosite – 0.2 fibres per ml when measured or calculated in relation to a 4-hour reference period.
(b) For dust consisting of, or containing, other types of asbestos but not Crocidolite or Amosite – 0.5 fibres per ml when measured or calculated over a 4-hour reference period.

A practicable code of conduct, based on the statutory requirements, would include the following precautions at the workplace:

(a) There must be an effective procedure for measuring the atmospheric contamination by asbestos dust or fibres, so that we know where we stand with regard to the Regulations and the precautions that need to be taken. Details are contained in Guidance Note EH 10, from the Health and Safety Executive, which describes sampling and measurement of airborne dust concentrations.
(b) Where practicable, other materials should be used in place of asbestos, so that the risk is reduced as much as possible. Where asbestos materials *have* to be used, they should be of the dust-suppressed, aluminised, or suitably bonded variety, so that dust generation is minimised.
(c) Asbestos products which are capable of shedding dust or fibres should be stored in special bins or containers, and these containers should be clearly marked to indicate that asbestos dust is dangerous to health. When dispensed from the stores, for use on the plant or workplace, such products should be placed in dust-proof wrapping.
(d) Plant and equipment used for work involving asbestos, and the working area (including storage areas), should be cleaned frequently to remove all traces of dust and fibres. Cleaning must be carried out by a method which does not generate or disperse dust – i.e. by effective damping down and wet brushing, or by using vacuum cleaning equipment fitted with disposable collecting bags and exhaust filters.
(e) Particular attention must be paid to jobs which involve the removal of lagging which contains asbestos. This operation can present complicated and costly problems to the average small or medium-size employer who may not have the facilities nor the experience to do it safely. It is advisable, therefore, to use the services of a specialist contractor who is qualified under the Asbestos (Licensing) Regulations 1983 (SI 1983, No. 1649). These Regulations place stringent controls upon the contractor's operating methods, and his activities are monitored by the Health and Safety Executive.
(f) Protective equipment must be of the type approved by the enforcing authority. Dust respirators which are approved under the Regulations are listed in Form F2486, Certificate of Approval (respiratory protection), obtainable from HMSO. Vaccum cleaners and dust extractors must meet British Standard 5415 Section 2.2, Amendment No. 4. Overalls must be of the type which will 'exclude asbestos dust', and must include suitable head covering.

Overalls used for working with asbestos must be stored separately from an employee's personal clothing, to prevent cross-contamination, and when sent for laundering they must be sealed in an impermeable bag and clearly marked to indicate that it is asbestos-contaminated.

(g) No work should be done with blue asbestos until the Health and Safety Executive Inspector has been contacted. He will require 28 days notice before the work begins.

The foregoing code serves only to offer advice on the treatment of asbestos in the workplace. To get the legal picture, managements will need to study the Regulations carefully. They show the seriousness with which the enforcing authority now views the asbestos problem.

As employers, we must appreciate that even small-scale operations which involve the handling of asbestos (particularly its application or its removal) must not be treated casually. Where smaller Companies lack the facilities or the expertise to cope with these operations safely, it would be wise to make use of experienced contractors who specialise in this line of business – with the provision that before any tender is accepted the contractor provides full information on the methods and safeguards he intends to adopt throughout the whole operation.

3.6 Threshold Limit Value (TLV)

The physical environment in which we live and work is subject to constant risk of pollution by a whole range of contaminants, from cigarette smoke to atomic waste, from discos to diesel fumes. As dedicated members of a consumer society we daily discover new ways to pollute the air we breathe.

The working environment must be maintained 'safe and without risk to health' declares the authoritative voice of HSWA – and who in his right mind would disagree with that! It follows, therefore, that where pollution is suspected or discovered there needs to be a way of measuring it, to determine whether the atmosphere is (or is not) safe and without risk to health.

The American Conference of Governmental Industrial Hygienists (ACGIH) publishes annually a list of chemical contaminants and indicates the concentration in air of these substances to which, it is believed, nearly all workers may be exposed day by day without adverse effect. The value of the airborne concentration of any of these listed substances is called its Threshold Limit Value (or TLV) and is measured in milligrams per cubic metre (mg/m^3) or parts per million (ppm).

The Health and Safety Executive periodically publishes this list in its entirety, as part of its Environmental Hygiene Series of Guidance Notes, and the published tables – together with explanatory notes and other information – are available from HMSO. (The current issue is entitled *Exposure Limits 1984,* Ref. No. EH 40, and became available in April 1984.)

TLVs, however, must not be regarded as being sharply defined points of division between 'safe' and 'unsafe' concentrations – they merely provide guidance on the levels to which exposure to a substance should be controlled in order to protect the health of the worker, based on five shifts of eight hours, over a 40-hour working week. On this basis, the TLV levels form part of the criteria used by the Health and Safety Executive in assessing compliance with the provisions of HSWA and other relevant statutory requirements.

The HSE emphasises that the best working practice is to reduce concentrations of all airborne contaminants as far below the TLV as is reasonably practicable. The warning is also given that because a particular substance does not appear on the published list, that substance is not to be regarded as 'safe'. Further, the application of the TLV to a particular situation should be interpreted by a trained occupational hygienist. The use of the TLV list, therefore, must be attended by a high degree of care and circumspection.

To complicate the issue, there are three categories of Threshold Limit Value:

(a) *Time-Weighted Average (TLV – TWA)* – the time-weighted average concentration for a normal 8-hour working day or 40-hour working week to which nearly all workers may be repeatedly exposed without adverse effect.

(b) *Short Term Exposure Limit (TLV – STEL)* – the maximal concentration to which workers can be exposed for a period of up to 15 minutes continuously, without suffering from:
    (i) irritation,
    (ii) chronic or irreversible tissue change,
    (iii) narcosis, of sufficient degree to increase accident proneness, impair self-rescue, or materially reduce work efficiency,
provided that no more than four excursions per day are permitted, with at least 60 minutes between exposure periods, and provided that the daily TLV – TWA is not exceeded. The TLV – STEL

should be considered a maximal allowable concentration, not to be exceeded at any time during any 15-minute excursion period.

(c) *Ceiling (TLV – C)* – the concentration that should not be exceeded, even instantaneously.

Some examples of TLV concentrations are shown below, and are included in Guidance Note EH 40

Table 3.1

Substance	TLV–TWA ppm	TLV–TWA mg/m³	Substance	TLV–TWA ppm	TLV–TWA mg/m³
Ammonia	25	18	Mercury	–	0.05
Arsenic	–	0.2	Nitric acid	2	5
Bromine	0.1	0.7	Nitric oxide	25	30
Calcium oxide	–	2	Octane	300	1450
Carbon black	–	3.5	Oxalic acid	–	1
Fluorine	1	2	Pentane	600	1800
Hydrogen sulphide	10	14	Sulphur dioxide	2	5
Lead	0.15	0.45	Zinc oxide	–	5

3.7 The Problem of Noise

Noise may be conveniently described as 'unwanted sound' – though this definition may be hotly contested by those who are progressively going deaf in their pursuit of ever-increasing amplifier power, at disco sessions: if they were asked to *work* in these noise levels, they'd go on strike!

Unwanted sound, then, is what we're talking about when we refer to noise, and it can be the roar of traffic in a busy town centre, the sound of someone's transistor radio in the quiet of the countryside, the cry of the baby next-door at two in the morning, or the shattering cacophony of sounds in a busy press shop or steel fabricating factory.

Noise – which is nothing more than sound wave pressure hitting the eardrums – exists at many levels, and is measured in decibels.

For the purpose of health and safety monitoring, we measure it over the frequencies which have the greatest effect on people, using units which are weighted to correspond to the hearing characteristics of the human ear, represented by the symbol dB(A).

People can suffer from noise in two ways – it can have a psychological effect, making people short-tempered and causing loss of concentration; or it can have a physical effect, which actually causes temporary or permanent loss of hearing, depending upon the intensity and the duration of exposure.

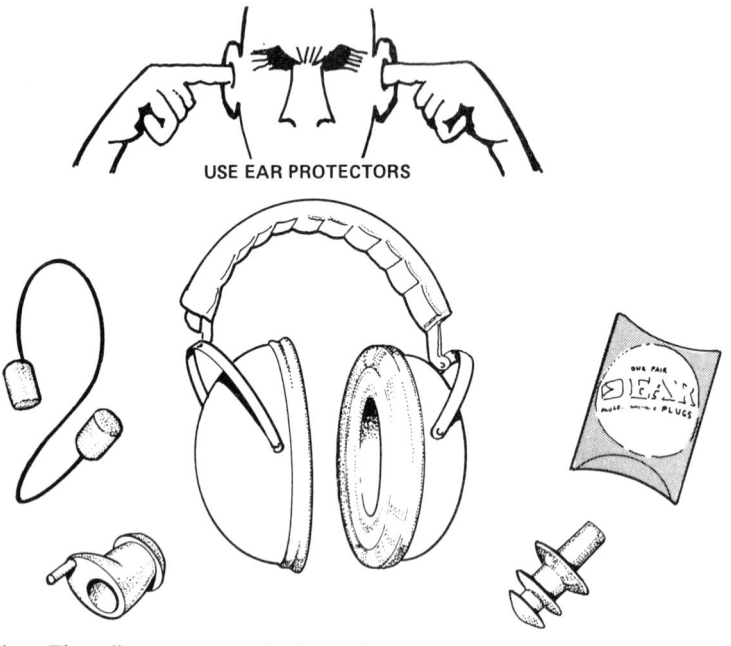

'... They all represent sound value ...'

The TLV for noise – the level to which the average person can be safely exposed for an eight-hour shift every week for a working lifetime – is currently set at 90 dB(A). Above that figure, he must wear ear protection or be exposed for a shorter period of time.

The intensity of noise does not increase on a simple arithmetic scale – it is measured on a logarithmic scale. thus, 100 decibels is not twice as loud as fifty.

The *Code of Practice for Reducing the Exposure of Employed Persons to Noise* (HMSO) illustrates the logarithmic relationship in its tables showing the maximum exposure time permitted, without the use of ear protection, for certain levels of noise (*Table 3.2*).

Table 3.2

Noise level, dB(A)	Exposure time
90	8 hours
93	4 hours
96	2 hours
99	1 hour
102	30 minutes
105	15 minutes

The above table shows that a person may be exposed to 90 dB(A) for a full working shift, but if the noise level is 93 dB(A), then he must be exposed for only half that time, and so on, *pro rata*.

The prevention of noise-induced hearing loss is accomplished in three ways. *First*, and best, the noise can be reduced to a safe level by initial proper design of the machine which is generating it; or by modification to existing machines, to reduce the noise they make; or by fitting effective sound-insulation to the source of noise; or by placing the noise source behind a suitable noise baffle, so that it's screened off from the populated workplace.

Second, by reducing the duration of a person's exposure to noise, by periodically stopping the equipment which generates it, or by removing the employee from the area during parts of the shift, so that he has 'noise-free' periods.

Third, by ensuring that he uses effective hearing protection, in the form of ear muffs, or ear plugs. (Cotton wool does *not* serve as effective protection against noise).

There are people who believe that when they've worked in a very noisy environment for any length of time, they 'get used to it'. This is a dangerous and often destructive myth. People don't 'get used to' harmful noise levels, any more than they get used to radiation or rat poison. The effect of high-level noise is a physical one and, as time passes, the hearing-loss which they suffer is progressive and measurable.

At the time of writing, the current Code of Practice specifies 90 dB(A) as the safe level. Future legislation on the subject will depend upon response to the currently available Consultative Document on 'Protection of Hearing at Work', which contains proposals for new Regulations plus a draft Approved Code of Practice and Guidance Notes. This document, together with a 66-page report of the HSE Working Group on Machinery Noise, are obtainable from HMSO.

Any manager who feels his area has a noise problem would do well to invest in a copy of each, and also in a copy of a useful publication called *Noise and the Worker*, issued by HMSO as No. 25 in the Health and Safety at Work series of Booklets.

They all represent sound value – no pun intended!

3.8 The Dust Problem

Dust is the other pollutant which we can sensibly do without at the workplace. Process-generated dusts still cause a lot of ill-health (and sometimes death) even though we know – or should know – their dangers.

The inhalation of dust of any sort can cause health problems. The degree of harm it causes relates to the degree of exposure, to the chemical composition or the toxicity of the material, and to the particle size of the dust which is inhaled.

For this reason Threshold Limit Values, applying to various types of dust, have been published by the Health and Safety Executive, and these are used as a guide for establishing safe exposure levels.

For the purpose of definition, let's say that *dust comprises particles of airborne material which remain in suspension for a sufficiently long period to be inhaled by a person in the course of his employment, and in concentrations likely to cause ill-health*. If this definition seems to apply to certain liquid mists, as well as to solids, then no harm has been done – cutting-oil spray in a workshop atmosphere, for example, must be treated just as warily as solid particles, and can be minimised by similar means.

Where it becomes evident – or is even suspected – that a particular workplace has a dust problem, there must be a systematic programme to deal with it. The programme cannot be carried through in its entirety by the manager alone; he will need technical assistance. But at least he can initiate the programme and can follow it through.

Depending upon circumstances, the programme will go something like this:

(a) *Sampling and Measurement* – to discover what sort of dust is causing the problem, and what scale of pollution is evident. This will need to be done by taking atmospheric samples at various places in the work area (or by means of 'personal samplers', carried by a number of selected employees) so that the dust burden in the air can be measured, to determine its concentration, and analysed to determine its composition.

An exercise of this nature is best carried out by competent people – the Company's Occupational Hygienist, if he exists, or perhaps an experienced member of the laboratory staff. Failing these two prospects, then the best course to adopt is a confession to the local HSE Inspector that a problem exists. He will arrange technical assistance or provide expert advice.

Other sources of advice are independent consultants, either in the field of industrial consultancy or maybe from one of the university engineering faculties.

In any event, it is necessary to know what the dust is, and how much of it is in the atmosphere. This will determine the courses of action which must follow.

(b) *Tracing the Source and Taking Action* – so that the fault can be located and rectified. Tracing the source should not be difficult – this is often simply a case of using one's eyes (together with a very high intensity light beam, if necessary) to seek out the leakage.

Curing or reducing the emission will be a different matter. There can be a whole range of causes – poorly designed plant, rotten sealing techniques, geriatric equipment, sloppy maintenance, bad working procedures, or maybe just careless and undisciplined employees. Again the manager might need assistance in dealing with the problem – from the design people, from the engineering department, from the man who has to authorise capital expenditure – but at least he must call upon these sources of help, and not let the problem fester.

Having discovered the cause of dust emission, the manager must eliminate it or take steps to reduce it to an acceptable level. This might involve a programme of effective maintenance, renewal of plant or equipment which has gone beyond salvation, the installation of dust-extraction equipment which removes the dust at a point close to its source, or perhaps simply a tightening of working procedures.

(c) *Specifying Personal Protection* – to stop dust getting into the employees' lungs. The first consideration must always be *prevention*. Where this fails, or where improvement methods have not achieved sufficient reduction, then we must fall back upon *protection*.

An employee who has to spend a large part of his day in a dust mask will not be happy in his work, and who can blame him!

However, where prevention has genuinely failed to make him safe, then a dust mask it has got to be.

There are many to choose from. Manufacturers like M.S.A., Siebe Gorman, 3Ms, etc. know their business and will be only too happy to advise and supply the *correct* equipment for the particular problem. The HSE Inspector, of course, will also be anxious to advise.

Once decided upon, however, the use of protective equipment must be supervised and strictly enforced – and in this stage of the game the supervisor is the man who must be relied upon to do his job properly. People tend to use all sorts of excuses, wiles, subterfuges and ingenious tricks to get out of their protective gear. We must be realistic about this – once the gaffer's back is turned, off it comes! Supervision is not easy – but it *is* essential. There may come a time when some learned judge will peer over his half-specs at the Company solicitor and ask gravely, '. . . and what *procedures* did the defendant adopt, to ensure that his employees actually *wore* the equipment provided?'

'. . . and what procedures did the defendant adopt, to ensure that his employees actually *wore* the equipment provided?'

One such procedure is to let the employees assist in making the choice of protective equipment. Consultation can pay dividends in achieving employee acceptance.

3.9 Scaffolding

For those people who have to request or use or erect scaffolding platforms in the course of section maintenance, these brief notes might be of assistance. Those managers or supervisors who have nothing whatever to do with scaffolding might still find the notes interesting, since they illustrate the standards of care which we have to adopt in order to protect employees from accidents.

Scaffolding platforms are both a means of access and a place of work, and the law demands that these shall be made and kept safe. The dangers are primarily two-fold – people falling off them, and things falling from them onto people.

Essential reading for interested parties is certainly *The Construction (Working Places) Regulations 1966 (SI 1966, No. 94)*, and in addition – for those who arrange for and supervise the erection of scaffolding – the British Standard Code of Practice No. 97, Part 1. For general guidance, Booklet No. 6D, in the Health and Safety at Work series, from HMSO, is very useful. Entitled 'Safety in Construction Work: Scaffolding', it deals with the subject in clear and unfussy language, and contains excellent simple diagrams.

What follows is a brief account of some of the requirements for minor scaffolds – the Regulations contain many paragraphs, dealing with many other aspects of scaffold safety, so that people who are responsible for the safe use of scaffolding should read and understand the Code of Practice and the Regulations.

Materials of construction

These must be sufficient for the job, and must be of suitable quality. Timbers must be in good condition and must *not* be painted. Metal parts must be free from corrosion, or from other patent defects which might affect their strength.

Erection

A competent person must inspect the materials on each occasion before they are put into use.

Erection, substantial alteration, additions and dismantling must be carried out by experienced people and must be supervised by a competent person.

Every scaffold must be rigidly connected to the building or structure which it serves, unless it is a properly designed mobile scaffold.

Drain pipes or chimney pots are not to be used as a support for any type of scaffold. Gutters or overhanging eaves must not be used for support, unless they are properly designed as walkways. Loose bricks or soft ground must not be used to support any scaffold platform which is more than 2 ft high – firm footing, such as base-plates on flat boards, must be used to distribute the load over the ground.

Structures used to support scaffolding

These must be sound, and must have firm footing. They must be adequately strutted and braced, to ensure stability. Uprights (or standards) must be vertical, or slightly inclined toward the building.

Ledgers (the horizontal tubes which are fixed to the vertical standards, over the *length* of the scaffold) must be properly horizontal and securely fastened to the standards by means of properly designed fittings.

Transoms (the horizontal tubes which span the ledgers, across the *depth* of the scaffold) must be securely fastened to the ledgers or the standards.

Putlogs (the horizontal tubes whose ends are used to secure the scaffold to the building or the structure) must also be firmly fastened to ledgers or standards.

Platforms

These must be closely planked, to prevent movement of the planks – though a space of 1 inch between planks is permitted, provided they are secured to prevent movement. Boards which are more than 2 inches thick must have a width of at least 6 inches. All other boards must be at least 8 inches wide.

No board shall project beyond its supports by a length which is more than four times its thickness, unless it has been properly secured to prevent it tipping if someone should stand on the end.

Every board must have three or more supports, unless it is short and thick enough to prevent undue sagging.

The maximum distance between supports (transoms) is determined by the thickness of the boards, according to the following table:

Table 3.3

Plank thickness	1¼ in	1½ in	2 in
Distance between supports	3 ft 3 in	5 ft 0 in	8 ft 6 in

Platforms must have secure guard rails, fitted to the inner side of the standards, which must be between 36 and 45 inches from the platform. Toeboards must be fitted along all the outer edges and the ends of the platform, and these must be at least 6 inches high. They must also be secured to the inner side of the standards. Space between the top edge of the toeboard and the lowest guard rail must not exceed 30 inches.

Width of Working Platforms

The minimum width of a working platform is determined by the purpose which it serves. The following table shows these minimum widths, though it must be emphasised that it might be necessary to exceed these statutory minimums if special circumstances arise wich make it sensible to do so.

Table 3.4

Purpose	Width (inches)
Access, and passage of materials, (footings)	25
Footings, and also for deposit of materials	34
For support of a higher platform	42
For dressing or rough shaping of stone	51
For supporting a higher platform and for stone dressing	59
Space between deposited materials and edge of platform	17

Access to platforms

Access ladders to any working platform must be firmly secured, so that movement is prevented. The top of the ladder must extend at least 3 ft 6 in above the stepping-off point.

Mobile Scaffolds

These must be set on level ground, and must be properly vertical. The wheels must be properly secured to the standards, so that they cannot drop out, and when a person is using the scaffold the wheels must be locked or effectively scotched to prevent movement.

The height, to platform level, must not be more than three times the base width if used out-of-doors, nor three-and-a-half times if used indoors. (When considering base width, this must include any outriggers which are used.)

A mobile scaffold must not be moved whilst any person is on its platform, and movement must be accomplished only by pushing or pulling at the *base* of the scaffold.

84 Sundry Subjects

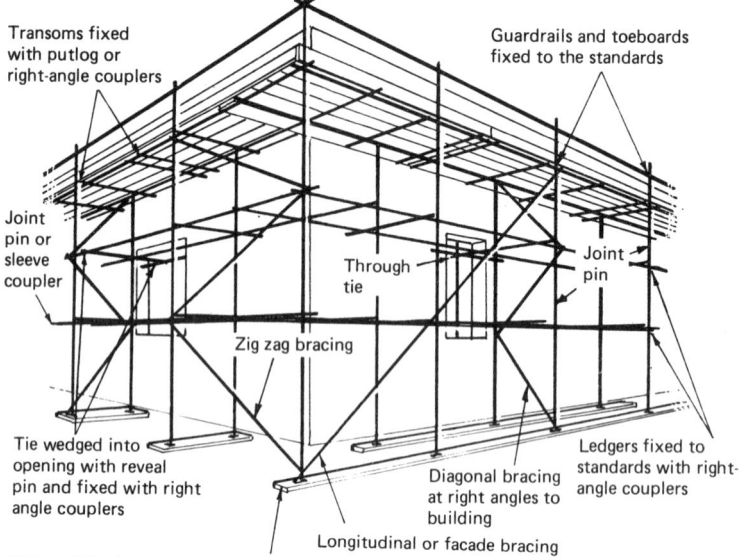

- Transoms fixed with putlog or right-angle couplers
- Guardrails and toeboards fixed to the standards
- Joint pin or sleeve coupler
- Through tie
- Joint pin
- Zig zag bracing
- Tie wedged into opening with reveal pin and fixed with right angle couplers
- Diagonal bracing at right angles to building
- Ledgers fixed to standards with right-angle couplers
- Longitudinal or facade bracing

1½ in x 9 in timber sole plates when standing on soil

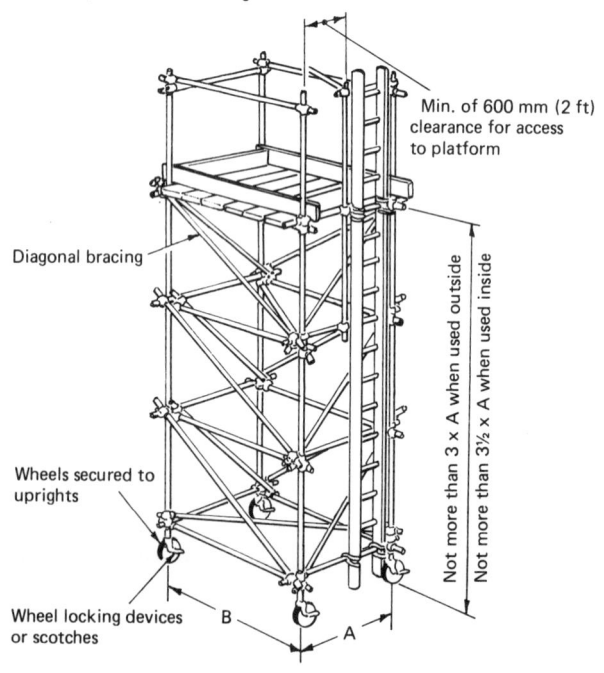

- Diagonal bracing
- Min. of 600 mm (2 ft) clearance for access to platform
- Wheels secured to uprights
- Not more than 3 x A when used outside
- Not more than 3½ x A when used inside
- Wheel locking devices or scotches

"Stability — Particularly for light weight scaffolds. Regard should be paid to stability either by adequately weighting at the base or by outriggers."

Corner standards should never be less than 1.200 m (4 ft) apart

Mobile scaffold constructed of steel tubes

Examination

Scaffolds must be examined by a competent person every seven days – or, additionally, after weather conditions which might have affected the strength or stability – and the record of inspection must be kept in the prescribed manner on Form F91.

Use of Scaffolds

Each employer whose employees use a scaffold must satisfy himself that it complies with the Regulations, whether it has been erected by his own employees or by someone else.

It is obvious, from the notes above, that the erection and use of scaffolding is not an enterprise to be undertaken lightly. Building a scaffold is a job for trained and competent people, and its use must be properly supervised. Before permitting his own people to use one, the manager or supervisor must be sure that the structure has been properly inspected and the inspection has been recorded in the register. He must also check the thing himself, to see the obvious features are in good order – its verticality, its patent stability, the handrails, toeboards, planking, means of access to the platform, etc.

Silly things can happen to a scaffold, during the time between weekly inspections. People sometimes steal planks for use elsewhere, or take away the ladder, or give the structure a careless (and usually unconfessed) nudge with a fork truck or lorry. The manager or his supervisor needs to recognise these nasty little 'modifications', when they occur, and to prohibit use of the scaffold until faults have been corrected.

Scaffolds which are damaged, or still in the course of erection, or being dismantled, must be clearly marked with a notice which prohibits use absolutely.

About eleven hundred people each year suffer lost-time accidents due to falling from scaffolds. The total may not seem astronomical, when said quickly, but remember that falling of a scaffold platform is not quite the same as falling out of bed!

3.10 Harmful Substances – Informing the Employee

There are so many chemicals, reagents, proprietary confections and other substances used at the workplace these days that it's almost impossible to list or keep track of them. Many of the proprietary ones have trade names which provide little indication of their true constituents, or what they contain in the way of harmful or dangerous chemicals. Though suppliers are now obliged to give information on the hazards of their products, many of them volunteer information which is so vague or generalised that it becomes almost useless.

'Do not swallow. If Cruddex enters the eyes irrigate well with water. Ventilate room during use', they say, or something equally non-informative. Trade secrets, perhaps, deter them from telling us whether Cruddex contains phenol, or hydrochloric acid, or carbon tetrachloride, or radioactive mustard gas, or any other interesting constituents. This is something we're perhaps not considered sufficiently responsible to know about!

Nevertheless, all employers of people are required to provide adequate information and instruction for their employees, so as to ensure their health and safety. (Have a look at Section 2.3.1.3 in Part 2 again – remember 'TITS'?)

The substances we expect people to handle – whether they're our products or someone else's – may comprise or contain flammables, toxics, poisons, acids, alkalies, carcinogens, irritants, anaesthetics, or any other category of harmful components. Our employees, therefore, must be given at least enough guidance to enable them to handle these substances safely. And unless we know exactly what chemicals they contain, we cannot provide this guidance effectively. It is not sufficient to know that we mustn't get it on our skin, etc. – we should know *why*.

To obtain sufficient information on a particular proprietary product is not easy, but neither is it impossible. If we use a particular brand of adhesive, or cutting oil, or filter aid, or colouring additive, or catalyst, or anything else, then we as *customers of the supplier* should be in a position to say,'Tell us what's in it, or we'll find an alternative product made by someone who *will* tell us!'

Having extracted sufficient information from the manufacturer or supplier, we must then have it evaluated by someone who can determine the hazards of the substance and can also give advice on how to deal with them. If the Company for whom we work is large enough, this can be done by a committee of informed people – like the Medical Officer, the Occupational Hygienist, the Laboratory Manager, the Safety Officer, the Production Manager, etc. If not, then advice can be obtained from the local Health and Safety Executive Inspector.

When formulated, this advice must be passed on to the employees who handle the substance; preferably in writing, and in a way which all concerned can easily understand.

This must be done for every substance which the employee has to use, and about which anyone has any doubts or fears. A large and laborious exercise, certainly, but one which is necessary if we are to carry out our legal and moral obligations to the employee.

A useful way of passing on this information is to produce a library of Material Data Sheets – one sheet for each substance – which can be kept always available at the workplace for instant reference. Ideally, every supervisor and every shop steward would have his own file of Data Sheets, and these files would be added to or up-dated as new information becomes available. The Data Sheet for each substance should contain the following information:

(1) The trade name of the substance or product.
(2) The chemicals which it contains, and in what proportions.
(3) What the substance is normally used for, and what it looks like.
(4) Its effect on the eyes, on the skin, on the respiratory system, or on any other parts of the human body.
(5) Any other known harmful effects, short or long term.
(6) Its Threshold Limit Value, if applicable.
(7) Whether highly flammable or flammable or combustible.
(8) *All* the precautions which must be taken when using it.
(9) Any first-aid measures which may be appropriate.
(10) How to dispose of spillage, waste, empty containers, etc.
(11) Any special instructions which might be appropriate.
(12) An assigned hazard rating, determined by the company.

This might appear to be an excessive burden on the shoulders of the employer. If you think this, spend a few minutes during each day of the next week just looking around your own patch, and list *all* the various products which you buy and which your employees have to handle. Having made the list, and hopefully looked at the label on each product, ask yourself if you know enough about each one to be absolutely sure of what it contains, of how hazardous it is (or isn't), of what the exposure effects are, of what precautions are necessary – and then ask yourself whether the employees know, too.

This is an exercise which will surprise you, and probably make you feel very uneasy!

3.11 Eye Protection

The eye is an organ of miraculous anatomical design. As an instrument of perception and expression it is unsurpassed. Leonardo da Vinci called it the window of the soul, and this is not too fanciful a description.

For our purpose, we must understand that a person has only two such windows to last him a lifetime, and that in most cases they are the key to his means of earning a living. A shade over 80% of the human eye is fairly well protected inside its cave of bone, but the bit that sticks out – the window of the soul – is very vulnerable.

The eye, given a fair chance, will last for a lifetime, but it can be damaged by excessive heat and light, by electromagnetic and ionising radiations, by aggressive chemical action, by mechanical abrasion and by physical impact. And there are very few working environments which contain none of these risks.

Further, these damage factors – heat, light, radiation, chemical, mechanical, physical – are only group headings. Within each of these groups lies a terrifying variety of specific hazards, any one of which can reduce a person's visual equipment by half, or destroy it completely.

The need to protect a person's eyes, therefore, is a vital one; as employers, we must ensure that we do all that is reasonably practicable to reduce the hazard, and that we take effective steps to protect the employee from the residue of hazard which remains. Prevention, followed by protection.

The statutory instrument containing the requirements for preventing eye injury is called, logically enough, *The Protection of Eyes Regulations, 1974 (SI 1974, No. 1681)*. It came into effect during April 1975, and it makes hard and fast rules for the provision of eye protection equipment to employees.

The following notes summarise the requirements of the Regulations; but again, the notes are by no means exhaustive – employers (and employees!) should read the Regulations carefully, to appreciate what full compliance amounts to.

In making provision for the issue of eye protectors to employees, two Schedules are appended to the Regulations. These schedules contain lists of operations which are hazardous to an employee's eyes.

Schedule 1 is divided into four Parts, and a total of 35 operations, or 'processes', are listed. Persons who are engaged for any part of the working day on any of the listed processes must be provided with approved eye protection equipment.

REFERENCES — REGULATIONS AND STANDARDS

The Protection of Eyes Regulations 1974, (S.I. 1974 No 1681), refer to the provision, maintenance and use of eye protectors in relation to certain listed processes and activities. This Code of Practice is additional to, and in no way seeks to minimise or modify, the provisions of the Regulations.

Where eye protectors are issued, these will conform to British Standards 2092, 679 or 1542 and their current amendments, and/or to that equipment listed in any Certificate of Approval issued by the Health & Safety Executive for the purpose of the Regulations.

DEFINITION OF "SUITABLE"

For the purpose of this Code of Practice, a person means appropriate to the risks encountered by the person carrying out a certain operation, and suitable for the person who is required to use the protective equipment provided. (In this context, close fitting Safety Goggles would be deemed suitable protection for a person working with a substance which is likely to sket or splash, whereas Safety Spectacles would not.)

In addition it must be recognised that protection must be provided — in the form of goggles, shields or screens, as appropriate — for persons other than those engaged upon the specified activities, who may be at risk from the activities as by-standers or passers-by. (See Section 2(h) and (i).)

DEFINITION OF EYE PROTECTORS

For the purpose of this Code of Practice, eye protectors include:

a) **Safety Spectacles,** having lenses and frames to the appropriate British Standard and fitted with side screens to afford protection against flying particles and dust. (BS 2092)

b) **Prescription Safety Spectacles,** as above with lenses manufactured to the prescription of a qualified optician for the sole use of the person for whom prescribed. (BS 2092)

c) **Safety Goggles,** manufactured to the appropriate British Standard, having ventilation buttons or ventilation slots which prevent the entry of splashed liquids. (BS 2092)

d) **Protective Goggles,** having coloured filter lenses for use during welding operations, whose filters conform to the appropriate British Standards (BS 679 and 1542).

e) **Face Screens,** having coloured filter windows for use during welding operations, whose filters conform to the appropriate British Standards, BS 679 and 1542. These may be designed to be hand held or to be worn by a person.

f) **Face Screens, or Visors,** designed to be worn by a person, to afford protection against flying particles and manufactured to the appropriate British Standard. (BS 2092)

g) **Secondary protection** against flying particles or welding operations may include the following:

h) **Fixed Screens,** to protect the operator against flying particles and machines, to protect against abrasive wheels or other machines, to protect the operator against flying particles and welding operations from flying particles or welding

i) **Portable Screens,** placed behind certain machines to protect passers-by from flying particles

j) **Portable Welding Screens,** placed around welding operations to protect passers-by from flash or glare

AVAILABILITY OF EQUIPMENT

It is the Company's intention to keep adequate stocks of suitable eye protection equipment, so that any reasonably foreseeable demand for such equipment can be promptly satisfied.

WELDING OPERATIONS

Protection of a person's eyes during welding, cutting or burning operations falls into two categories.

a) **The person carrying out the operation,** who will be wearing the appropriate goggles or face screen as a protection against arc eye, or intense light from a gas welding operation. In addition, he will also be required to wear suitable protection against flying particles which might arise from the subsequent chipping or dressing of a completed weld.

REPORTING EYE INJURIES

It is the duty of all employees to report to the Medical Department without delay when any job-related injury to the eyes occurs, or when an eye problem exists on site, such as the safe conduct of his duties.

Where first-aid measures have been taken on site, a prompt using an eye-wash bottle or safety shower, must be made for subsequent visit to the Medical Department for examination and possible further treatment.

b) **The by-stander, or passer-by,** whose eyes might be affected by flash or glare from a welding operation. In this case, the by-stander should be provided with safety spectacles or goggles having light-filtering lenses, and these should be worn throughout the welding operation.

In the case of passers-by, protection should be afforded by erection around the area of portable welding screens. These screens should be so placed, and be of sufficient height and opacity, to effectively prevent the transmission of electric arc flash from the welding operation to the eyes of a person passing by.

Where contractors are carrying out welding or cutting operations within the Refinery, their operations should be screened, and liaison between the contractor and the Engineer ensure the

CODE OF PRACTICE
for the selection, provision and use of
Eye Protection Equipment

10 The handling, in open vessels of dangerous or corrosive substances, either liquid or solid, where there is a reasonably foreseeable risk of damage to the eyes from skets or splashes and the breaking up of crystals in open containers where a similar risk is present.

11 The breaking, cutting, dressing, drilling or similar working by means of hand-held or power operated hand tools, of the following: hard or similar substances, tiles, glass, firebrick, plaster hard plastics, concrete, where there is reasonably foreseeable eyes from flying fragments.

12 The use of compressed air for removing dust, dirt or shavings or similar material from

13 The cutting of wire or similar material from there is a forese

14 W

FIRST-AID EQUIPMENT

For the purpose of this Code of Practice, first-aid equipment refers to eye wash bottles, safety showers, eye wash fountains and any similar or related equipment which may be provided for use.

It is the Company's intention to supply a sufficient number of these items so that emergency eye-wash treatment is available at those places where eye injuries are reasonably foreseeable.

Such equipment should be conspicuously marked for ready identification, and access to it must be kept unobstructed at all times.

Eye wash bottles should be contained within protective boxes, mounted on a wall or a stanchion at about shoulder height, and the box should have a hinged front which is easily opened by means of a stout handle.

The bottle should be of a proprietary brand, fitted with a spray eye bath protected by a removable cap and capable of being operated by squeezing the bottle.

'... ignorance of the law is no defence ...'

Schedule 2 contains a further five listed processes. Where these processes are being carried on, the employer must provide protection for persons who may be at risk from, though not employed in, the listed processes.

The type of eye protection to be provided is specified in the following manner:

Schedule 1 – Operations listed in Part 1 of the Schedule require 'eye protectors', which are described as goggles, visors, spectacles or face screens, 'being equipment made to be worn by a person'.

– Operations listed in Part 2 of the Schedule require 'a shield, or a sufficient number of fixed shields'. A shield is described as 'a helmet or hand shield, being equipment made to be worn, or held by a person'. A fixed shield is described as 'a screen which is free-standing or which is made to be attached to machinery, plant, or other equipment'.

– Operations listed in Parts 3 or 4 of the Schedule require 'eye protectors, or a shield, or a sufficient number of fixed shields'.

Schedule 2 – Operations listed in this schedule require the provision of 'eye protectors, or a shield, or a sufficient number of fixed shields' in the case of one listed operation, and 'a sufficient number of fixed shields' in the case of the other four operations.

'Eye protectors' provided in pursuance of the Regulations must be *given into the possession of* those persons who are working on the listed processes, and should they become lost, destroyed, or defective, then the persons must be given replacements. In addition, the employer must keep a reasonable stock of spare eye protectors, so that he can comply with the Regulations.

The protective equipment provided must conform with the approved specifications for such items – that is, the appropriate British Standards – and must be marked in such a way as to indicate the purpose for which they are designed. And when made to be worn by a person, it must be 'suitable' for that person, as well as being suitable for the risk envisaged.

Persons for whom eye protection is provided *must use* such protection whilst employed on the operations listed; must take reasonable care of the equipment; must report loss, damage or defect – and must not wilfully misuse it.

It will be seen from the foregoing that the Regulations place an onerous duty of care on the employer.

The forty-odd operations listed in the two Schedules have not been included here, for a good but perhaps cruel reason – people concerned with the safety of employees will now, hopefully, be encouraged or persuaded or even frightened into buying a copy of the Regulations, in order to study them properly and then set up the necesssary procedures for full compliance.

Sufficient to say that there will be very few workplaces which don't contain at least *some* of the processes listed. So if you don't already have a copy of the Regulations, get one without delay. The cost is very small, compared with the potentially awful price an employee might have to pay for neglect on the part of his Company. And remember that ignorance of the law is no defence, when the Inspector comes knocking on the door.

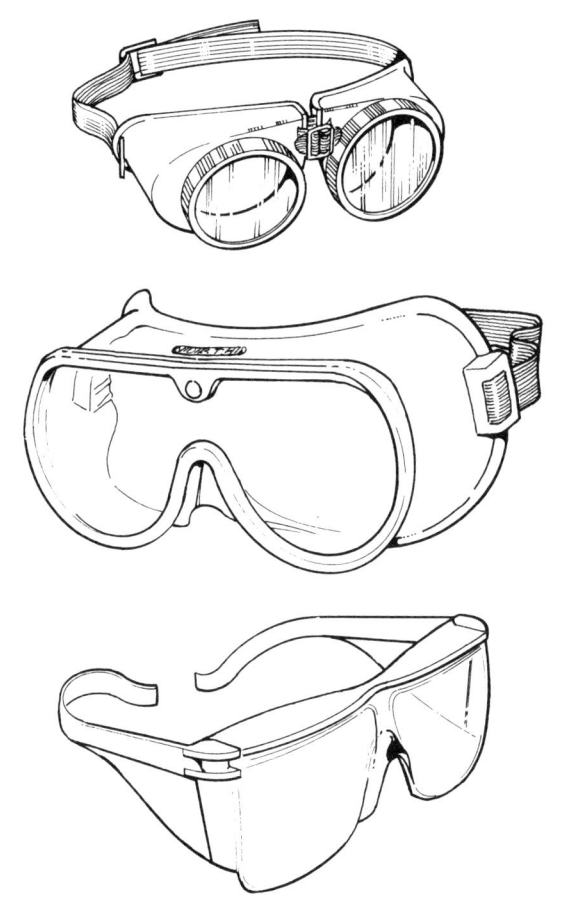

'. . . must be suitable for that person, as well as for the risk envisaged . . .

There is another aspect of eye protection, in addition to the provision of defensive equipment, which is worthy of inclusion in the Regulations. For some reason best known to the draftsmen it never had a mention. So let's try to repair the omission.

In the best regulated workplace, and in spite of goggles, visors, screens and other protective gear, *someone* at *sometime* is going to get a splash or a piece of something in his eye. He will need to find a ready source of clean water, to wash it out again before going for medical treatment. This implies a sufficient quantity of safety showers, or eye-fountains, or eye wash-bottles, strategically placed near the likely source of danger, so that he doesn't have to run about the workplace, half blind and probably in pain, searching for a wash basin or a water tap.

The equipment provided will depend upon the type of risk inherent in the process, but there are few working areas where nothing at all is required.

Where acids, strong alkalis or other corrosive liquors are used in any quantity, a safety shower is essential, supplemented by several eye-wash bottles.

Where the risk is sufficiently scaled down, then perhaps eye-wash bottles only are necessary. These must be placed where they can easily be seen and reached by a person in trouble. Their locations must be conspicuously marked – preferably by using the approved proprietary pictogram safety signs – and there must be an established routine for checking the bottles at the start of every day or shift, to ensure that the bottles are full of clean water.

The most convenient eye-wash bottles are the proprietary eye-bath-and-spray type, made of flexible plastic, with a flip-off cap over the eye-bath. They should be kept in dust-proof cabinets which are easily recognisable, highly accessible, and sited close to the source of danger. Nothing else must be kept in the cabinet. (There is a case on record where a routine inspection revealed two identical bottles in an eye-wash cabinet. One was the real thing; the other contained a concentrated detergent solution, used for testing joints in a gas main, left there by some idiot because he 'wanted somewhere handy to keep it'!)

The thing about eyes is that people only have two, as we noted earlier, and they're not transplantable. Loss of one, or both, is one of life's major tragedies. Whether it's television, a football match, a sleek pair of legs, or a blood-red sunset over a shimmering lake which forms your ideal scenic turn-on, try to imagine life without it – then go out and review your arrangements for eye protection!

3.12 Fire Extinguishers

The chemistry of fire is elegantly simple. Before a fire can start, and in order for it to survive, there have to be three components present – fuel, heat, and oxygen. Remove one of these, and it won't start or it will go out. This is the basic truth illustrated by what is commonly known as the 'Fire Triangle' – a simple device which helps us to remember the formula.

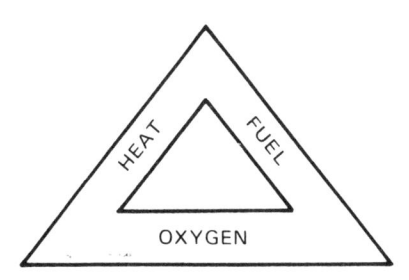

The design of all fire-fighting equipment is centred on the fact that once the triangle is broken, extinguishment results.

Complication sets in, however, when we have to decide which limb of the triangle to attack, and by which means.

Removing the fuel can be simple enough (or impossible, depending upon circumstances!) – it can be raked away, or kicked onto the garden path if it's just a few cardboard boxes or a pile of smouldering weeds. If it's a jet of burning hydrogen, or a blazing rivulet of naphtha from a leaking pipe flange, then it might be possible to shut off a supply valve further up the line. The fire is thus starved of fuel, and it dies.

Removing the heat or the oxygen is a matter for exercising choice over the available fire extinguishers, and the wrong choice could leave you without a place of work to come into next morning.

There are five basic types of fire extinguisher, and the manager/supervisor – and the employees whom he controls – must know how to find them, how to choose the right one for the job, and how to use it effectively.

Let's look at each of them in turn, and confirm that we really do know what we think we know.

Water extinguishers – painted red, and usually containing two gallons of water, propelled from the nozzle by gas pressure. The modern ones have a dip-tube which extends almost to the bottom, and a striker-knob on the top. Remove the protective cap from the knob, thump the knob hard with the flat of your hand, and a carbon-dioxide cartridge is pierced. This pressurises the water inside the container and forces it up the dip-tube and out through the nozzle. Use the extinguisher upright, and direct the jet of water into the seat of the fire – and keep on squirting until the extinguisher is empty. A water extinguisher can be used on fires involving carbonaceous materials – cardboard, paper, wood, fabrics, etc.

It must NOT be used on electrical fires, nor on fires involving liquid fuels.

Water is used to cool the fire – to remove the 'heat' component from the fire triangle.

Foam extinguishers – painted cream, and usually containing two gallons of foam solution. Activated in the same way as water extinguishers, but used for extinguishing fires involving *contained* flammable liquids – in small open tanks or other vessels. When the knob is struck, a jet of foam squirts out from the special nozzle and can be sprayed gently onto the surface of the burning liquid.

The technique is to aim the jet at the rear wall of the vessel, just above the surface of the liquid, so that the foam is able to splash off the rear wall and flow toward you across the surface. This lays down a blanket of foam, which smothers the fire by cutting off the air from the liquid surface.

Do *not* squirt the foam directly into the liquid – it will simply disappear beneath the surface and the blanket won't form.

Do *not* use foam on 'free-flowing' liquids – it will just be carried away by the liquid and will disperse.

Do *not* use foam on electrical fires, since it comprises mainly water.

You will see, from the foregoing, that foam is a somewhat specialised extinguishant, used to best effect on liquids which are contained in open vessels.

Dry powder extinguishers – painted blue, and varying in size from 5 lb nett up to about 50 lb nett. These are very effective against fires involving flammable liquids, oils, greases, fat, and can also be used safely on electrical fires since the powder is a non-conductor.

The powder is discharged by CO_2 pressure (either from a CO_2 cartridge or by a 'stored pressure' of gas, inside the cylinder), which forces the powder up a dip-pipe and out from a nozzle. The smaller units have a 'fish-tail' nozzle on the shoulder of the cylinder; the larger ones have a short length of hose with a hand-grip valve on the end. Once activated, the smaller extinguishers discharge all their powder; the larger ones, however, can be started and stopped by squeezing or releasing the hand-grip.

To activate them, slip off the protective cap (or the clip) from the striker knob, then thump the knob. Hold the extinguisher upright, and squeeze the hand-grip. Fan the fire with the jet of powder, sweeping the fire away from you with side-to-side motions whilst advancing from front to back.

With the smaller units, keep at it until all the powder has been used. With the larger ones (fitted with a hand-grip), it is possible to stop, if the fire appears to have been killed, and have a look; if any small areas are left burning, or if re-ignition occurs, the hand-grip can be squeezed again to release more powder for a second attack.

Dry powder is a smothering agent, primarily, though there is also thought to be some chemical interference with the combustion process. In the right hands, a dry powder extinguisher is an excellent weapon.

Carbon dioxide (CO_2) extinguishers – painted black, and containing liquid carbon dioxide under pressure. Activated by withdrawing the locking pin from the handle and squeezing the hand-grip. This releases the carbon dioxide via a tube which terminates in a horn-shaped outlet. The gas emerges in a flossy cloud, to the accompaniment of a hissing banshee scream which can frighten the living daylights out of the inexperienced or unwary operator – so be prepared for it!

Use the jet of CO_2 in the same way as dry powder, and on the same types of fire – flammable liquids, oils, etc., and on electrical fires. Good for electrical or delicate electronic equipment, since CO_2 is a clean gas which leaves no residual mess – unlike dry powder, which covers everything in a white blanket!

When discharging a CO_2 extinguisher, use one hand for the hand-grip (also a stop-start valve), and use the other to direct the horn outlet. But be sure to hold the horn by the rubber handle at its narrow end, otherwise it's possible to suffer 'frost-bite' from contact with the horn itself, which becomes extremely cold due to a rapid drop in temperature associated with sudden vaporising of the CO_2 liquid.

Vaporising liquids extinguishers – painted green, and containing a liquid which vaporises, on expulsion, to form a jet of inert gas. Used for the same types of fires as CO_2 and dry powder.

These are usually rather small units, and very useful for domestic use, or for fires on car engines or electrics – and therefore have the disadvantage of being attractively portable and easily stolen from their workplace locations! Otherwise excellent for dealing with small fires in enclosed places. Can be squirted into openings in electrical gear, cabinets, under car bonnets, etc. After use, however, the room should be well ventilated to disperse the vapour.

Activation methods vary somewhat, but usually there's a locking pin or tab to pull off, and a hand-grip to squeeze.

It becomes plain that it is *not* sufficient to grab the nearest extinguisher and just blast away at a fire. The right one has to be selected, and it has to be used skilfully. There are labels on extinguishers which describe their contents and their method of operation, but when a fire breaks out there is little time for light reading!

The thing to do, therefore, is to:

(a) ensure that the appropriate type of extinguisher is placed where it can do most good (and least harm), so that one doesn't have to spend time wondering if it's the right one to use;

(b) become familiar with the colour code, and with the instructions on the label, so that you *know* what it contains and how it works;

(c) ensure that a few employees in your department are as well versed as you are – because when the fire breaks out you'll probably be at a meeting, or in the toilet, or gone for tea, and there won't be time to send for you to deal with it.

Other points to be pondered and acted upon are:

(d) Arrange a system of regular inspections, to ensure that extinguishers are in good condition and are always where they should be – not used as door-stops, or coat hangers, or for other peculiar purposes.

(e) Ensure that they are conspicuous, with a pictogram sign on the wall above which indicates their location from a fair distance; and ensure that access to them is kept clear of obstruction at all times.

(f) Ensure that your department is equipped with a sufficient number of them – if one fails to go off, there won't be time to go to the stores for another. One extinguisher hanging on the wall in splendid isolation is perhaps cosmetically pleasing, but there is a real need for back-up units.

(g) – And once an extinguisher has been used, get it recharged or replaced immediately. There's nothing quite so dead as a dead extinguisher!

Just a few additional notes on fire extinguishers, to modify the advice where appropriate.

Some extinguishers have CO_2 cartridges which supply the pressure to expel the extinguishant. These units are fitted with striker-knobs, which drive a pin into the seal at the top of the cartridge. Others are already pressurised by the manufacturer or the service agent, and the 'stored pressure' is indicated by a pressure gauge fitted to the body of the unit. These don't have striker knobs. (But check the pressure gauge, during inspections, and have the unit serviced if the indicator shows pressure below the recommended level.)

Carbon dioxide (CO_2) extinguishers, as well as vaporising liquids ones, can be hazardous if used in a small enclosed room. CO_2 is an asphyxiant, and care must be taken to ventilate the area after using such a unit.

A fire extinguisher or a water hose reel is an efficient 'first strike' weapon in the hands of an experienced, confident person. Those people who are inexperienced or less confident, however, should never place themselves at risk by indulging in amateur heroics. The Fire Service will not thank anyone if they think they've been called in too late to do any good, or if they have to search for charred bodies in a burned-out building because of delay in sending for professional assistance.

If there are any of the old-fashioned carbon tetrachloride extinguishers lurking in odd corners of the workplace, they should be disposed of immediately. Carbon tetrachloride is *not* a safe liquid extinguishant, since it gives off harmful fumes, particularly when in contact with hot metal.

3.13 Fire Alarms and Evacuations

Safety law is concerned with the preservation of life, rather than property, and its requirements are geared to this philosophy. The Factories Act and the Fire Precautions Act don't demand the provision of 'sufficient and suitable means of fighting a fire' in order to protect the shareholders from financial loss if the factory burns down – the idea is to stop people getting roasted in premises which could catch fire for want of 'suitable means' to stop it happening.

For the same reason, the law demands a Fire Certificate, which carries details 'as to means of escape in the event of fire'. It also demands that people shall be made *familiar* with the means of escape, and that there shall be a suitable warning device which signals the event of fire. Hence fire alarms and fire exits, and hence the requirement to test fire alarms at intervals not exceeding three months.

The most practical way to satisfy these requirements (and also to satisfy the purely moral obligation) is to operate a procedure for routine testing of fire alarms and to tie this in with routine fire-evacuation drills.

Written procedures are essential and, depending upon the size of the premises and the number of people employed, these can either be posted in places where people can readily see them, or they can be given to each individual employee. The procedure should spell out the policy and requirements for alarm tests and evacuation drills, making it absolutely clear that nobody is excluded or excused from taking part.

In those premises which have alarm systems, the performance of a test/evacuation takes surprisingly little time – the interruption of a meeting or a tea-break for a few minutes every three months is a very small price to pay for the benefits which accrue.

To include a model procedure in these notes would be of little value, due to the huge diversity of conditions found in different workplaces, but all procedures should share the following basic features:

(a) A note on where the fire alarm activation buttons are situated in the particular workplace, and instructions on when and how to activate the alarms.
(b) Instructions on where to assemble, following evacuation, so that a 'head-count' can be carried out by those who have been designated as fire wardens.
(c) Where appropriate, instructions on the shutting down of any equipment during the course of evacuation, but only if this is essential to safety and only if it can be done without placing a person at risk in doing so.
(d) A list of nominated fire wardens, together with a note of their duties in the event of evacuation.
(e) An emphatic instruction that *everybody* is to evacuate the premises when the alarm is given, whether they know that it's a practice drill or not, and that they're not to stop to pick up handbags, coats, portable radios or any other items of personal

equipment – the drill is to ensure smooth and speedy escape from danger, not to protect trinkets.

(f) A note on who should be responsible for contacting the fire team and/or the outside fire services, immediately subsequent to evacuation, so that this can be done promptly in a case of actual need.

(g) Instructions for re-entry of the premises, after completion of the drill.

Having initiated such procedures it's useful to keep records of performance, so that their effectiveness can be monitored. Modifications or improvements might be necessary, based upon observation of the drills by a manager with a stop-watch and an eye for trouble.

It's also useful to set traps for the complacent ones among us, like putting a temporary notice on one of the exits which indicates that the way out is blocked. This teaches escapees to ring the changes on escape routes, and encourages people to 'think on their feet'. (On this subject, people should be trained to walk swiftly to the fire exit, during a fire evacuation. Running can cause panic, and if the front runner trips we can be faced with a pile of injured bodies on the stairs or jammed against the exit door. It's happened on too many occasions.)

And on the subject of escape routes, the law demands that 'means of escape' shall be clearly marked as fire exits by an appropriate and conspicuous sign. Whilst any person is working in a building, doors which afford a means of escape must not be locked from the outside, nor fastened from the inside in such a manner that they cannot be quickly and easily opened by a person making his way to safety. Blocked fire exits are an abomination, and it is the employer's duty to maintain exits which are clear of obstruction and easily accessible. And a final word on exits – a passenger lift is *not* a means of escape. People have been trapped in lifts, during fires, and have died there!

3.14 Fire Prevention

The prevention of fire is, like the prevention of any accident, largely a matter of anticipating problems, of inspecting the workplace with a trained and suspicious eye.

Storage of flammable substances; proper maintenance of electrical equipment; planning of 'hot work' in sensitive areas; designation of 'no smoking' zones; attention to small detail; enforcement of proper procedures; – all these comprise a package of fire prevention measures.

Good housekeeping is an essential segment of the programme, since untidiness and rubbish-heaps breed fires in addition to disease and disgust. The biggest fires, the real devastators, usually have small beginnings, and the speed with which a small fire in a pile of rubbish can grow into a conflagration is alarming.

Preventing the *spread* of fire, and its by-products of smoke and fumes, is also vital. A closed door can be a very effective temporary barrier against spreading flames or a marauding smoke cloud. Keep them shut, especially when the building is vacated at the end of the day. And fire-stop doors in corridors are there for a purpose – the practice of chocking them open or tying them back is sheer lunacy. More people are killed by smoke suffocation than by the flames of a fire, as any fireman will confirm.

The basic rules apply to factories and workshops, just as they apply to the more self-contained areas such as warehouses, stores, laboratories, offices, contractors' huts, and anywhere else where people gather to earn their living. They protect life and preserve jobs.

(a) If you smoke, make sure there are plenty of large ashtrays available – stub out cigarette ends carefully, and don't leave half-smoked cigarettes on the edge of the desk. Break matchsticks in half, before tossing them in the ashtray – it's an old woodsman's trick, to make sure they're not still burning. Don't throw the contents of ashtrays into the waste bin without a very careful check – and never less than half-an-hour before leaving the premises.

(b) Litter breeds fire, so put all your waste paper into the litter bin. Waste paper *baskets* won't contain a small fire – and if you have any in use anywhere, get rid of them and use metal bins.

(c) Electric fires with open radiant elements are not really suitable for workplaces, but if you have one make sure that it's positioned well away from anything combustible. Keep clothing away from heaters – clothes or papers placed on the vents of convector heaters can cause a fire, due to a stoppage of circulation and rapid build-up of heat.

(d) Switch off all electrical appliances when not in use, and remove plugs from their sockets. Don't overload circuits by running more than one appliance from any one socket, unless an electrician has certified that it's safe to do so. Be alert to the danger of damaged switches, sockets, plugs, cables, etc., and report these without delay.

(e) Keep all flammable liquids in closed containers, to avoid spillage. There are approved cabinets available for storing containers of highly flammable liquids – assess your need for these, and get enough of them for safe storage of solvents, thinners, cleaning fluids, and any other flammable liquids in use.

The prevention of fire at the workplace is a primary component of loss control, and is very much a part of management's responsibilities.

3.15 Office Safety

Though the following comments are written under the heading of 'Office Safety', they can be applied equally to other working areas – safety precautions are universal. Office managers and staff, however, might feel neglected if not specifically included in these pages. What is worse, they might think that offices are 'safe' by comparison with the harsher world of work outside. This is not true; working in an office or a laboratory can prove hazardous, too.

Working in an office is not always as safe and orderly as people think. Roughly 5000 lost-time accidents occur in office premises every year – in addition to the much larger total of minor bumps and bruises which cause no lost-time, and which are therefore not included in the annual casualty list published by the Chief Inspector of Factories. Activities among the teacups and typewriters may not have the drama associated with factories, blast furnaces, construction sites and coal mines, but the risk of accidental injury is nevertheless always present.

Slips and falls account for almost half of all office accidents. They are caused by simple, silly things like trailing electric cables, worn or turned-up carpets, spilled liquids turning polished floors into skating rinks, worn stair treads, tattered floor mats, boxes of stationery left in walkways, and similar unsafe conditions created by unsafe people.

A common cause of falls is the iniquitous habit of standing on a stool (or even a swivel chair!), to reach up for something. Stools, chairs and corners of the desktop are *not* regarded as safe means of access. If things *have* to be stacked out of normal reach, then a suitable set of portable steps must be provided and its use insisted upon.

Undignified and often bruising results can also be obtained by running, rather than walking. Alacrity is a virtue, but it's difficult to imagine an office situation which calls for anyone to go pounding down the corridor at a gallop. Nothing can be *that* urgent – not even one's response to the office fire alarm.

Remember, also, that whilst very high heels are extremely sexy and attractive (on a lady, at least!) they may not be suitable for the busy office. Shoes can be fashionable *and* safe, if chosen wisely; conditions and activities at the place of work should govern the choice of style.

Furniture and fittings can be a cause of accidents, when designed or arranged or used by people. Look around you, as you sit at the desk or walk through the office, and seek out the potential for injury which lurks among those innocent trappings of office life.

Can you cross the floor without gouging your thigh on the corner of the desk? Is the route strewn with awkwardly placed cabinets, waste paper bins (*not* baskets – they burn too easily!), telephone tables, coat racks, etc? Can you open the drawer of the filing cabinet without cracking your elbow on the adjacent wall? Maybe a little rearrangement would make things more convenient, or safer to move around. There might even be some items which you don't really need, and which would leave you with more space if they were disposed of.

Remember that filing cabinets can be unstable and may topple if badly loaded, or if a fully laden upper drawer is left open. It makes sense to put the heavier files in the bottom drawers, where possible, to provide ballast; and a quite narrow strip of wood placed under the front edge of a cabinet will lend just enough backward tilt to make a big difference to its stability. Oh, yes – and do you *really* need that pot of flowers on the top, which can fall onto your foot?

Lifting and handling accidents are by no means rare, in offices. Muscular strains and painful backs, squashed fingers, aches and pains, typewriters dropped onto unprotected toes – these can easily be the penalties for incorrect lifting and handling methods. People should be taught the basics of this commonplace activity, so that they don't have to learn the hard way:

(a) If the load is on the floor, bend your knees and keep your back straight – lift by using your thigh muscles to raise yourself and your load – *don't* bend your back.
(b) Keep the load close to your body – don't carry it with your arms outstretched.
(c) Make sure you can see where you're going, over the top of that thing you're carrying.
(d) If it's too heavy for you, don't struggle with it – get someone to help.

These are (or should be) quite well known and simple rules for painless lifting and handling – a little persuasion and a little practice can help to reduce the toll of back injuries.

Electricity can kill – the layman must *never* tamper with electrical equipment in the office, or anywhere else. If plugs, sockets, switches, cables, etc. need repair or attention, leave it to the electrician whose job it is to do these things. Unauthorised persons must *not* fiddle with electricity – faults must be reported promptly to the maintenance supervisor. This includes even the simple blown fuse in a three-pin plug, since a fuse doesn't blow without a good reason and the reason should be investigated by a qualified craftsman. People who pull out dead fuses and insert bits of wire, hairpins, etc. in their place are inviting a fair degree of heat build-up and other problems, somewhere in the circuit. (A fearsome example of this sort of meddling involved a badly charred plug, too hot to touch and smelling strongly of burning plastic, which was found to have a small brass woodscrew in place of the fuse. Lord preserve us from the enthusiastic amateur!)

Horseplay – practical jokes – fooling around – or whatever else it may be called – has caused many injuries at the workplace; and offices are no exception. The victim rarely finds it amusing and the perpetrator has nothing to laugh about, either, when the 'joke' backfires and becomes a tragedy. Judges and Factory Inspectors take a dim view of clowning which results in personal injury, and there have been prosecutions which demonstrate their attitude toward this.

The workplace is not the venue for horseplay.

Offices, shops, laboratories and other similar premises in which the noise and drama of the factory may not exist – these have their share of accidents, too. We have to be aware of this, and exercise due care and vigilance to sort out the unsafe acts and unsafe conditions.

A useful pocket-size booklet, suitable for individual issue to office staff, is published by RoSPA; it's entitled *Care in the Office* (Ref. No. IS/109) and is packed with illustrations and good advice.

3.16 Last Round-up

These notes have been designed to provide some basic guidance on accident prevention and the legal requirements relating to health and safety at the workplace.

They are aimed primarily at the manager or the supervisor, since these are the people who can do most to achieve a successful Company performance in this important field. They also offer guidance to all other 'persons at work'. What has been presented here is nothing more than a series of short essays, touching on commonsense precautions and the basics of accident prevention philosophy. An effort has been made to avoid solemnity and jargon, and to include only the more widely relevant aspects of safety, so that the material presented will be useful to the broad base of employers and employees.

As far as the legal notes are concerned, they must not on any account be seen as exhaustive, or even approaching completeness – they scratch the surface, and even then not very deeply. The purpose of the notes is to provide a flavour of the legislation which surrounds us, and to encourage appropriate people to do the requisite reading for themselves. This is essential, for ignorance of the law's requirements can lead to serious trouble for employers and their emloyees.

In considering accident prevention, the definition of the word 'accident' should be fixed firmly in our minds – we are looking at *potential* consequences, rather than the actual ones. Remove the *cause*, before the effect becomes manifest. And let's not see bloodshed as a prerequisite; damage is also a result which can arise from the unplanned event which we call an 'accident'. Loss control is therefore the total objective.

As management people, we owe our *Company* a duty of care, as well as owing it to our employees; our endeavour and our responsibility extend both ways, upward and downward.

Don't shy away from seeing accident prevention (i.e. loss control) as an aid to profitability. Accidents cost money, and reducing costs improves profit – and there's nothing reprehensible in profits, for without them there wouldn't be a Company in which to be a manager or an employee.

Appendix 1
Commonly Used Acts and Regulations
(available from Her Majesty's Stationery Office – HMSO)

The Factories Act 1961.
The Offices, Shops and Railway Premises Act 1963.
The Fire Precautions Act 1971.
The Health and Safety at Work etc. Act 1974.
The Highly Flammable Liquids and LPG Regulations 1972.
The Asbestos Regulations 1969.
The Protection of Eyes Regulations 1974.
The Safety Committees and Safety Representatives Regulations 1978.
The Notification of Accidents and Dangerous Occurrences Regulations 1980. (To be updated)
The Construction (Working Places) Regulations 1966.
The Factories Act 1961 etc. (Repeals) Regulations 1976.
The Woodworking Machines Regulations 1974.
The Abrasive Wheels Regulations 1970.
The Safety Signs Regulations 1980.
The Control of Lead at Work Regulations 1980.
The First-Aid at Work Regulations 1981.

Appendix 2
Useful Reference Publications

British Standards Institution, 2 Park Street, London WIA 2BS:

BS 5908:1980 – Fire Precautions in Chemical Plant.
BS 5378:Part 1:1980 – Safety Signs and Colours.
BS 4275:1974 – Selection, Use and Maintenance of Respiratory Protective Equipment.
BS 5304:1975 – Safeguarding of Machinery.
BS 2890:1973 – Specification for Troughed Belt Conveyors.
BS CP 97:Part 1:1967 – Metal Scaffolding.
BS 2092:1967 – Industrial Eye Protectors.

Her Majesty's Stationery Office (HMSO), 49 High Holborn, London WC1V 6HB (and from Government Bookshops):

Section List No. 18 – Health and Safety Executive Forms and Publications.
Health and Safety at Work Booklets (by HSE), as follows:

No. 4   – Abrasive wheels.
     5   – Cloakroom. Accommodation, etc.
    6D – Scaffolding.
   18   – Industrial dermatitis.
   19   – Safety in laundries.
   21   – Drilling machines.
   22   – Dust explosions in factories.
   25   – Noise and the worker.
   33   – Guillotines and shears.
   35   – Basic Rules – Safety and Health.
   41   – Woodworking Machines Safety.
   42   – Horizontal milling machines.
   44   – Asbestos – health precautions.
   50   – Welding and flame cutting.

(NB There are others, listed on the back cover of each booklet.)

Code of Practice for reducing the exposure of employed persons to noise.

Safety Representatives and Safety Committees (Regs, C/P and Guidance Notes).

Guidance Note EH40 – Occupational Exposure Limits, 1984.

Approved Code of Practice – Control of lead at work.

Health and Safety Commission Newsletter (published bi-monthly – details from Area Offices of the Health and Safety Executive).

Guidance Notes from the Health and Safety Executive (on a variety of subjects under the headings of Medical, Environmental, Hygiene, Chemical Safety, Plant and Machinery, General). – List from the Health and Safety Executive, Baynards House, 1 Chepstow Place, London W2 4TF.

Appendix 3
Journals and Other Sources

Journals

Health and Safety Information Bulletin – Industrial Relations Services, 67 Maygrove Rd, London NW6 2EJ.

Safety Surveyor – Victor Green Publications Ltd, 106 Hampstead Rd, London NW1 2LS.

Protection – Alan Osborne & Associates Ltd, 6 Tranquil Passage, London, SE3.

Health and Safety at Work – McLaren Publishers Ltd., Davis House, 69–77 High Street, Croydon CR9 1QH.

Occupational Safety and Health – RoSPA (see below).

Risk and Safety Management – British Safety Council (See below).

The following bodies are useful sources of information, advice, publications, charts and posters, etc:

Royal Society for the Prevention of Accidents (RoSPA) – Cannon House, The Priory, Queensway, Birmingham B4 6BS.

British Safety Council – 62/64 Chancellor's Rd, Hammersmith, London W6 9RS.

Fire Protection Association – 140 Aldersgate St, London EC1A 4HX.

Appendix 4
Safety Signs

U.K. membership of the European Economic Community has led to a new Statutory Regulation which requires the standardisation of safety signs throughout member countries. All new safety signs must therefore comply with a modified British Standard, in terms of design, shape, colour. Signs fall into four categories, according to the message they carry:

Prohibition – things which, for safety reasons, you must not do, (e.g. 'No Smoking'). A red circle with a diagonal bar through it.

Warning – indicating a particular hazard which you must be aware of, (e.g. 'Danger – fork lift trucks'). A black-edged yellow triangle.

Mandatory – something which, for safety reasons, you **must** do, (e.g. 'Wear eye protection'). A blue disc, with a pictogram on it.

Conditions of Safety – indicating the location of fire exits, emergency showers, eye wash bottles, etc. A green square or rectangle, with a pictogram or legend on it.

All newly erected safety signs have to conform to the standard, and all existing signs must be replaced by January, 1986.

Appendix 5
Safety Inspection Checklist
Unsafe Acts – Unsafe Conditions

Machine Guards
  Are all dangerous parts properly guarded?
  Are guards in good condition?
  And properly secured?
  Can a person touch any dangerous part of the machine?
  Or reach through any feed opening in the guard?
  Are interlocks working properly?

Stacks and Storage
  Do stacks restrict access?
  Or safe visibility?
  Are stacks properly bonded and stable?
  Are they too high?
  Do they encroach beyond floor markers?
  Has removal of drums/bags created instability?
  Is there safe working space for trucks?
  Is there any fire risk?

Vehicles
  Are unauthorised passengers being carried?
  Is the speed limit being observed?
  Is the driver taking due care?
  Is the vehicle being used for its designed purpose?
  Are there any obvious defects:
    Tyres
    Klaxon
    Seats
    Lighting
    Steering
    Braking
    Safety fitments
    Exhaust

Roadways
    Are there dangerous pot-holes or irregularities?
    Or oil patches?
    Or loose objects/obstructions?
    Are traffic signs plainly visible?
    And not missing, or damaged?
    Are road markings plainly visible?
    And adequate/suitable for the circumstances?
    Is lighting adequate?
    Are essential routes properly indicated?
    Are existing barriers, fences, markers in good condition?
    And being properly respected?
    Are temporary hazards enclosed/marked/lighted?
    Are pavements obstructed or damaged?

Working Areas
    Is good housekeeping satisfactory?
    Are walkways clear, and in good condition?
    Are there handrails on stairs?
    And kicking strips on platforms?
    Are stair treads in good condition?
    Are portable steps/stools in good condition?
    Is lighting satisfactory?
    Are there 'objects liable to fall'?
    Are there tripping hazards?
    Or slipping hazards?

Means of Access

    Are all ladders safe?

        All rungs in good condition.
        Both stiles intact.
        No 'patent defects'.
        Feet OK where fitted.
        Sensibly stored.
    Are ladders being used safely?

        Correct angle – (4 up, one out) – i.e. about 75°.
        Properly secured at the top
        Or firmly 'footed' whilst in use.
        3 ft–6 ft above the landing point.
        Correct length for the job.

Scaffolding
    Materials in good condition.
    Fully planked out.
    Handrails fitted.
    Toeboards fitted.
    Standards firmly based,
    Properly vertical to the ground,
    Tied to the structure.
    Provided with tied access ladder,
    Platforms wide enough for the purpose.
    If Mobile: – wheels locked,
              not higher than three times its width,
              set on level ground,
              wheels secured to uprights.

Hand Tools
    Are they properly chosen for the job?
    Are handles in good condition?
    Are heads mushroomed?
    Are jaws spread?
    Are they proper tools, not makeshifts?
    Are they safely stored?
    Are they in good condition generally?

Power Tools
    Are they properly guarded?
    Electrical leads O.K.?
    Any obvious defects?
    Is the person trained to use it?
    Is it being used for its proper purpose?
    Are they properly stored?
    Is there a noise or dust problem?

Harmful Substances
    Do we know what it is?
    And what the hazards of use are?
    Is it properly contained?
    Is the container labelled?
    Are there safety codes which apply?
    Are these being observed?
    Is there spillage/leakage?
    Are tanks/vessels adequately covered?
    Or their edges higher than 3 ft–6 ft above floor level?

Is protective clothing specified?
And being worn?
Are there showers or eye-wash bottles conveniently near?
Is it carried/transported safely?
Are bunds, gutters, drains, etc. in good condition?

Fire Precautions
Is there a fire risk from –
  rubbish, debris?
  'solid' substances in use?
  flammable liquids?
  flammable gases?
  hot work or processes?
  electrical equipment?
  heating, smoking, 'cooking'?
Are flammable liquids properly stored?
Are 'minimum quantities' kept in workrooms?
Are precautionary notices displayed?
Are suitable extinguishers provided?
Is there free access to extinguishers?
Are they conspicuously placed?
Are means of escape kept clear?
Are fire exits marked?
Are fire-stop doors kept closed?
Are fire exit doors unlocked?
Are fire alarm buttons unobstructed?

General
Are safety notices legible?
Is good housekeeping satisfactory?
Is safety equipment available?
And conspicuous?
Are people using protective clothing?
And not taking obvious risks?
Are hygiene factors satisfactory?

(*Note.* This is by no means exhaustive; it merely provides examples of what should be looked for during inspections.)

Index

Absolute duty, 41, 62
Accident,
 definition, 6
 classification, 16
 notifiable, 27, 49
 Report form, 23
Amosite, 71
Automatic guards, 63

Chrysotile, 71
Competent person, 69, 81, 85
Crocidolite, 71

Dangerous occurrence, 27, 48, 49
'Dangerous part', 63, 110
Dust masks, 80

Entry permit, 43
Employers' liability, 34

'Fire triangle', 93
Flash point, 67, 68, 70
Frequency rate, 13

Guardrails, 82, 111, 112
Guidance notes, 74

Hazard rating, 31

Incidence rate, 13

Induction training, 61

Loss prevention, 9

Manual handling, 43, 102
Material data sheets, 87

Permit to Work, 43
'Practicable', 41
'Prime Mover', 62

'Reasonably Practicable', 40, 41, 62, 88
Responsibility, employee's, 3, 50
Risk evaluation, 10, 41
Robens Report, 38

'Safe by position', 62
Safe systems, 43
Safety audit, 29
 inspection, 30
 sampling, 29
 survey, 29
 tour, 29
Self Regulation, 38, 39

Transmission machinery, 62

Unfenced machinery, 65
Unsafe acts/conditions, 19, 21, 101, 103

Welfare, 41, 46